The Rising Sisterhood

Rise With Us: How to Step Into Your Own Power & Change Your Narrative

Compiled by: Amy Edge

Contributors:
Jillian Bright, Michele Duhigg, Felicia Ford, Giselle Grant, Kayleigh Hanlin, Hannah Hassler, Charmaine Johnson-Fuller, Cassie Kitzmiller, Erin Klein, Lucy Liu, Christine Lu Singh, Tonia Rolle Jones, Rachel Smets, Kacie Steinmetz, and Sharon White

Illustrated by: Madison Edge

The Rising Sisterhood © Copyright 2021 by Amy Edge

ISBN: 9798592509841

"Embodied" © Copyright 2021 by Hannah Hassler
"Grit" © Copyright 2021 by Amy Edge
"Faith" © Copyright 2021 by Jillian Bright
"Awakening" © Copyright 2021 by Sharon White
"Unburdened" © Copyright 2021 by Tonia Rolle Jones
"Fighter" © Copyright 2021 by Kayleigh Hanlin
"Confidence" © Copyright 2021 by Rachel Smets
"Decisions" © Copyright 2021 by Giselle Grant
"Triumph" © Copyright 2021 by Michele Duhigg
"Unapologetic" © Copyright 2021 by Christine Singh
"Abundance" © Copyright 2021 by Charmaine Johnson-Fuller
"Dream Again" © Copyright 2021 Cassie Kitzmiller
"Freedom" © Copyright 2021 by Lucy Liu
"Tenacious" © Copyright 2021 by Felicia Ford
"Connection" © Copyright 2021 by Kacie Steinmetz
"Reinvention" © Copyright 2021 by Erin Klein

All rights reserved. No part of this publication may be reproduced, distributed, or transmitted in any form or by any means, including photocopying, recording, or other electronic or mechanical methods, without the prior written permission of the publisher, except in the case of brief quotations embodied in critical reviews and certain other noncommercial uses permitted by copyright law.

Adherence to all applicable laws and regulations, including international, federal, state, and local governing professional licensing, business practices, advertising, and all other aspects of doing business in the U.S., Canada, or any other jurisdiction is the sole responsibility of the reader and consumer.

Neither the author nor the publisher assumes any responsibility or liability whatsoever on behalf of the consumer or reader of this material. Any perceived slight of any individual or organization is purely unintentional.

The resources in this book are provided for informational purposes only and should not be used to replace the specialized training and professional judgment of a health care or mental health care professional.

Editor: Lauren Smulski
Illustrator: Madison Edge
For more information: hello@therisingsisterhood.com

If you've ever felt invisible, this book is for you. We see you. You matter. Our sisterhood unites us to rise and support each other as we strive toward our dreams.

Table of Contents

Introduction

The Movement

Section 1: Overcoming the "Less Than" Story We Often Tell Ourselves

"Embodied" by Hannah Hassler	15
"Grit" by Amy Edge	25
"Faith" by Jillian Bright	37
"Awakening" by Sharon White	47
"Unburdened" by Tonia Rolle Jones	55

Section 2: Giving Yourself Permission to Step into Your Power

"Fighter" by Kayleigh Hanlin	63
"Confidence" by Rachel Smets	73
"Decisions" by Giselle Grant	81
"Unapologetic" by Christine Lu Singh	91
"Triumph" by Michele Duhigg	103

Section 3: Showing Up in Your Life to Unlock the Impact You Can Create

"Abundance" by Charmaine Johnson-Fuller	117
"Dream Again" Cassie Kitzmiller	129
"Freedom" by Lucy Liu	139
"Tenacious" by Felicia Ford	147
"Connection" by Kacie Steinmetz	157
"Reinvention" by Erin Klein	171

Write Your Own Story

A Special Thanks to Our Contributors

Acknowledgements

Introduction

"There is no greater agony than bearing an untold story inside you."

—Maya Angelou

This book is a compilation of essays from sixteen women who decided to rise, overcome their struggles, and cultivate a life of impact. These stories are not unique, but each author has crystallized her own message and is bringing you along on her journey. It is my hope that you will see something of yourself in their struggles and be inspired to take action, so that you, too, can rise.

The Rising Sisterhood has taken many months to compile and has undergone many different versions since its inception. Its original idea was a calling, then the "idea" marinated and began to unfold into a magnetic pull. And now, this book has engineered a movement—a movement to craft a space for women to share their stories.

It has long been my dream to create a platform that will inspire women to "decide to rise" above the struggles, the adversities, and the boxes we tend to lock ourselves into. With *The Rising Sisterhood*, I feel that we have not only created a space for these remarkable women to share their stories, but also a way for other women to see that they are not alone. We are rising together.

There is power in our shared circumstances, and as a community, we need to honor those shared experiences, empower each other, and celebrate when we overcome our adversities. As you are reading these stories, I hope you take inspiration from the many ways in which these women have freed themselves from the shackles of circumstance. You, too, can be freed from these shackles, if you decide your story is bigger than this moment.

You are meant for more. And your story is meant to be told.

The Movement

"Your story is what you have, what you will always have. It is something to own."
—Michelle Obama

This is more than a book. The Rising Sisterhood is a community built upon the notion that every sister deserves a safe place to feel welcomed, celebrated, encouraged, and lifted up, as we all rise and change our own narratives.

Our community is part of a larger movement. This movement goes beyond us; it is intended to be a vessel for serving others in our community and our world. It is our goal to not only provide a platform for women to tell their stories, to be seen, to be heard, and to be understood, but also to serve others.

This is why, each year, the net profits from this book will be donated to a charity. In 2021, we will be donating to the Trevor Project. (For more information, visit thetrevorproject.org.)

Our sisterhood inspires us to rise and support each other as we strive toward our dreams, and I want to personally invite you to join us, to rise with us. If you'd like more information on how to share your story in our next book, you can find that information here: www.therisingsisterhoodbook.com/coauthor.

Section 1

Overcoming the "Less Than" Story We Often Tell Ourselves

"Owning our story and loving ourselves through that process is the bravest thing that we'll ever do."

—Brene Brown

Have you ever told yourself a story of how you are "less than" someone else? This is simply a false narrative that we create within ourselves, but that inner critic can paralyze our efforts to move our dreams forward. The constant comparison game robs us of our happiness, and if you decide to keep playing it, that game will keep you from fulfilling your purpose and reaching your goals.

But if you are determined to reach success—which I know you are!—you must decide to revise the current "story" you are playing on repeat in your head. Those who realize their dreams are the ones who, despite their troubles and hardships, will eventually cross the finish line, even if that means crawling their way to completion.

Don't let the stories of others pull you off your path to greatness. Your story is uniquely yours, so walk forward with confidence and determination, and never forget your vision.

Don't wait for permission to start living your dream—begin today!

Embodied

by Hannah Hassler

I grew up being the "smart" kid. Not popular. Not funny (in public, anyway). And definitely not well dressed. I wasn't the girl anyone was trying to get fashion tips from, and you wouldn't have been asking to borrow my lipstick in the ladies' room. In fact, I have a vivid memory of seeing a picture-perfect girl working out at the gym once (hair on point, trendy outfit, full face of makeup) and, while I was puffing away, dripping sweat and feeling my hair frizz out by the minute, I idly said to someone within earshot, "Wouldn't it be amazing to look that good just to go to the gym?"

She gave me the once-over and said, "Well, that could happen if you were to actually *try*."

Yes, I was that girl. And honestly, no one would have accused me of even being interested in trying to steal the spotlight. I was used to being the behind-the-scenes, make-you-look-good, unsung-hero-of-the-backstage type. Some of that came from growing up with religious traditions that made it abundantly clear that women had a place, and it was *not* as leaders or frontliners. My own internal desire to make things perfect (yes, I'm an Enneagram 1!) definitely played into it; after all, backstage is a great place to obsess over details without risking the public shame of making a mistake.

Some of that came from a belief that I wasn't good enough to actually *be* the main attraction. The good news, according to me, was that I liked it that way. That's not even sarcasm—for the longest time, I believed (and lived) the idea that I didn't want to be seen, heard, or noticed. I told myself I liked being the master puppeteer and running things from behind the curtains.

Until one day, when I woke up in a (metaphorically) tiny box: no light, no air, no room to move. I felt literally backed into a corner on every level—personal, professional, you name it. I was trapped in what seemed like every conceivable way.

On a personal level, I was living a solid thirteen-plus-hour drive from my dearest friends and family. My husband and I were knee-deep into the infertility journey, and I was exhausted by a body that just wouldn't work, doctors who didn't seem to have a clue what PCOS was (much less how to treat it), and hormones that were wildly out of whack. Not surprisingly, my depression was surging back around, and I also ended up with a thrilling case of stress-induced IBS. It was not my finest hour.

Professionally, I was teaching in a Texas middle school that had some really wonderful points...and some problem areas. Dealing with the long hours and state testing pressure, plus the ongoing meetings, student behavior issues, and school politics would have given me a run for my money even in peak health, but I was far from feeling my best. The hormonal issues, depression, infertility, and IBS were a lot to deal with, so I tried to just focus on serving and investing in my students. Unfortunately, that wasn't quite enough. I started having panic attacks every time I was in a silent, empty classroom—not that such a thing happened very often, but I desperately wanted to use those moments for peace, not panic!

Even through all of that, I kept up my "I'm here to serve you and of course I never need credit" shtick. I was on committees. I volunteered at my church. I went to school early, stayed late, and showed up on weekends. If there was a way to backstage myself, I did it. My name was rarely on anything, because I was never the ringmaster. I created a life in which I didn't have a voice, because I was always handing the mic off to other, "more qualified and deserving" people.

I didn't have room to grow, expand, or change because I required myself to be who people *wanted* me to be, and who I told myself people *needed* me to be. I couldn't have told you how I liked things, because that was never an important criteria for me. I didn't know what my own desires were, because they never mattered when I was serving everyone else. I had people who loved and cared about me, of course, but they didn't really have a reason to think that I wasn't all right, especially when I made such a point of voicing how much I *wanted* to play the roles I allowed myself to play.

Eventually, I began to see the writing on the wall. Things were falling apart, and they weren't going to get better if I kept pretending it was all fine. I found a counselor, and I swore to myself that I was going to focus on *me* (in an earlier foray, I had explored how easy it is to talk about everything *but* the reason you're really there), and I started showing up. Every week, for fifty minutes, I learned to talk about the life I was living, and what it meant to have a voice, to take up space, and allow myself to be *me*, without the constraints of what anyone else needed, wanted, or expected.

I found out that a lot of the "rules" I had been living by weren't coming from anyone other than myself, and that I had a whole lot more freedom than I had ever allowed myself to acknowledge, much less use. And, in a funny twist of fate, I realized that I wasn't actually afraid of the bad things that might happen in my work or life. Really, I was more afraid of the good things. In fact, much (dare I say most) of my fear, angst, worry, apprehension, and general trepidation in this life wasn't actually about failing. Rather, it was about being successful, being seen, and being known.

I came to understand that I wasn't sure how to actually take up space in my life and world (*thanks, counseling!*). I didn't know how to metaphorically—or even literally—speak in a clear voice that would be heard and responded to. The concept of rising up, becoming known, and living a life of success felt...foreign. I could visualize and accept failure, smallness, and minimizing myself all day, every day. *That* I knew on an intimate level, it seemed.

But success...success was the vast unknown that scared my socks off. So even as I said I wanted it—that I desired to leave teaching and start my own business, author a book, launch a podcast—*a part of me very much did not want it at all.* And that's the part of me (of all of us, really) that I needed to invest some extra time into; the part that would prefer to fail because it's ever so much safer than dreaming big and risking success. As I gathered my courage, I surveyed the cramped quarters and stale air that seemed to constantly surround me, and I decided to begin breaking free, no matter the cost, risk, or uncertainty.

Some tools and practices that have helped me push past my current reality and begin to embody a fuller sense of my own desires include reading *The Artist's Way* by Julia Cameron, walking and sitting meditation, attending counseling, and doing The Work (established by Byron Katie). My favorite practice, and one that has helped me tremendously in the process of moving away from fear (and learning why I was so set on avoiding success in the first place!), is the Deepest Fears Inventory. This is something I read about in Carolyn Elliot's book, *Existential Kink*. My personal practice is a bit different than the book version, but it's very much inspired by her work. One of the best things about it is that while it's not fancy, I've come to understand so much about myself, my desires, and my personal blocks with just a piece of paper, something to write with, and a few spare minutes.

Here's what I do (feel free to join in!): I choose something in my life, business, or world that I've said I wanted or expressed a desire for, but that has never happened. This is stuff like the tired-out New Year's resolution I add to the list every year (looking at you, "get in shape"), and of course those things that aren't really resolutions so much as dreams I've carried around for more than a minute. Things like writing a book, performing improv, traveling overseas, buying a house, and starting a business. We all have our things we carry around.

Once I have my focus, I grab a piece of paper, write out the following statement, fill in the blanks with my dream/desire, and brainstorm fifteen to twenty reasons to fill in that blank line after my *because*:

I absolutely refuse to _____ because _____.

Here are a few statements I've done the inventory with. Often the first things that come to mind are pretty surface level, as you'll see!

I absolutely refuse to write a book because…I'm afraid no one will read it.

I absolutely refuse to lose weight because…that would mean no more Reese's cups.

I absolutely refuse to charge more for my services because…it might be harder to get clients.

Pretty basic stuff, am I right? But *then*, once I get past about ten or so, the real feelings come out to play. I find myself getting real and pulling zero punches.

I absolutely refuse to write a book because...I won't have any control over who gets to read it and what they will think about me as a result.

I absolutely refuse to lose weight because...excess weight is my only "easy-to-see" PCOS symptom that doctors seem to take seriously.

I don't want to charge more for my services because...I don't want people to expect even more of me than they already do.

Those real feelings are powerful. When I write them, I always recognize right away that I'm on to something, because I can feel it in my body. At this point, I've done a lot of these inventories, and I've seen some patterns emerge. For example, not being able to control things is really scary for me. (Surprise! Widespread success on a large scale means you won't be able to control a whole *lot* of things!) Being seen and heard is something I say I want, but the reality of being seen and heard overwhelms me and makes me want to slink away. And at the end of the day, being small is something I equate with being safe.

These were some of the things that had started coming to light in my counseling sessions as well; things that kept me wading in the shallow end, helping other people make their dreams a reality while I comforted myself with platitudes about how lovely it was to be safe in the shadows. I realized that a large, secret part of myself was not on the same page as the part of me that was talking about my dreams for success. And no matter how loudly I said I wanted to make more money…to grow my business…to author a book…to be an authority in my field…none of that would ever have a chance to happen if the truth remained, down in my core, that I did *not* want those things at all. The truths we hold in our bodies and our minds play a pivotal role in the lives we are able to lead out in reality.

When we say we want something that doesn't ever manifest, we must ask ourselves what other truths may be contending with the words we're speaking. What are our bodies revealing? What are our minds tripping against in the dark? How much do we want to know the answers? If we allow ourselves to explore that inner reality, we can begin to identify areas we would like to address, ideas we would like to shift, and beliefs that no longer serve us. All of this can lead us into more fully embodying the light and truth we wish to be in the world. And according to my friend Merriam-Webster, embodiment is "the representation or expression of something in a tangible or visible form."

As you begin to explore your own desires, to sit in the stillness, and to push against your previous boundaries, the process of tangibly expressing your true Self will begin. You'll connect with your own passion in a visceral way, and you'll gain more clarity on what truly matters to you. You'll begin to see yourself as a full person, with the right to take up space, to have a voice, and to pursue your dreams fully. You will finally begin to live the fullest reality of yourself.

Instead of creating ever-smaller compartments that you deem "safe enough" to eke out an existence within, you must be willing to stretch and expand; to lean into your deep, core truths and desires. This can feel frightening and overwhelming at first, especially if you've created a life around limitations and avoidance! One way to combat this is to be extremely intentional about practices like meditation, journaling, and counseling. Also, let yourself feel your feelings—maybe just an edge at first, as much as you can handle before you have to turn away. Then, little by little, with intentional practice, you can increase your ability to feel BIG things, to understand hard truths, and to embrace your wildest desires. By choosing to return to your body and to be fully present, you can more easily align your desires and your reality, which is the core of what embodiment is all about.

This is your one life—and allowing yourself to tangibly represent and express the woman your soul is calling you to be is the best gift you can possibly give yourself.

About the author: Hannah Hassler is a former teacher turned entrepreneur and impact creator. She has served as a strategist, writer, and course creator in the six- and seven-figure businesses of entrepreneurs, authors, and world-changers, and especially loves working with women who have big dreams. She has also served as a one-on-one coach for new entrepreneurs.

Hannah is currently earning her MA in Psychology and Creativity Studies, as well as an Integrative Wellness Coaching Certificate, from Saybrook University. She has written several academic papers on embodiment, intersectionality, and social entrepreneurship.

Her current passion project is to create a collective community for women who desire to be the tangible *embodiment* of what they say they believe as they learn to *express* themselves authentically and powerfully and *expand* with ease.

You can find her latest project at hannahhassler.com.

Grit

by Amy Edge

Let's go back—not *way* back, but to the time when I felt the most uncomfortable in my skin. The awkward years of middle school. I was rocking the dork look in those days: the large glasses and the ultra-high bangs, and the clothes that tried to be in style, but were somehow always less than those of my classmates. If I had been a nerd back then, maybe it would have made sense, but I was only getting by with Bs. My perfectionist self was never thrilled with that subpar performance, but striving to be better only ever seemed to cause more shame and disappointment.

There's not one single moment I can pinpoint as the precursor for those feelings of discomfort and inadequacy. Rather, they seemed to stem from many small events that happened over time. I was constantly belittled by the other students at school, to the point where walking the halls and hearing the comments and condescending remarks directed toward me felt like being stabbed over and over.

It's funny, though—while many of the kids took their shots, there's only one girl whose insults I vividly remember. I can still hear her voice whenever I begin to doubt myself. I remember her name and her piercing expression as she scolded me. I'm not sure why I was her "chosen one," or what I ever did to earn my status as her punching bag. Maybe there wasn't a single "thing." Perhaps she just needed someone to be the brunt of her jokes, or the girl to point her finger at and have the rest of the crowd join in.

They were relentless, and the harmful words often went deeper than my outward appearance, aimed directly at my character instead. Those comments hurt the worst.

"I can't believe her family even likes her."

"No wonder her dad left."

"She's barely gonna make it to graduation. I hope she slits her wrists."

Those words began to sink in, and eventually, I believed them. They became my truth. I began to discount my worth as a person, and grew to assume that I was *less than*. Less than everyone else around me. In fact, I believed I was nothing. I was occupying space that I didn't deserve. I didn't have anything to offer—any talents or gifts I'd once had were now nothing more than a fleeting thought.

It didn't matter if I tried to excel—the echoing feeling of worthlessness continually grew. Each time I made a considerable effort to befriend someone, they quickly abandoned me. Whenever I raised my hand in class, I was mocked. And if I made even a slight effort to improve my appearance, I was laughed at.

So, I stopped trying. What was the point?

Some nights I laid in bed and thought, "What if I just left? It's not like anyone would really care or notice."

But still, I stayed. I trudged on. Even though every day felt more hopeless than the last.

***

Walking the halls of the school was tortuous. I dreaded every moment between classes, but I went through the motions and pretended to be "okay." I kept my head down and tried to become as invisible as I could. I put on a smile for my family and masked the pain.

And, for the most part, I fooled everyone. I even began to fool myself, and gradually accepted that this soul-shattering feeling was just the way it was meant to be. This was just the way *I* was meant to be.

This was just my life.

Sure, I had hopes, dreams, and passions, but they were never aligned with what my circle of adults, peers, or family believed was possible for me. Why waste time and effort on dreaming, when in reality, I wasn't worth breathing the same air. So, I never attempted to pursue anything. I never tried a little harder. I never gave more effort.

I went through middle school and into high school just getting by. Going through the motions and always plastering a smile on my face. Looking around at everyone else, I never felt like I belonged—like I was accepted.

I felt like a fraud.

I *was* a fraud.

Halfway through high school, I realized I had to give a bit more effort. So, I decided to just pretend—pretend to be another person. It was basically my only option if I wanted some semblance of a life, or any kind of relationship with the people I saw each day.

I learned how to push down the pain. My armor was pretty tough by then, and I was mostly numb to the insults thrown at me. I built myself up and created a shield around my feelings. I tried new things, and on the outside, I seemed to be happy. I made the high school cheer team. I had a group of friends that I socialized with. I went to school dances. I did all the things that a typical teenager would do.

But my opinion of myself continued to decline. I knew I wasn't really being *me*, and that made liking myself an impossible feat. It only got worse as time went on—as I flocked toward the people who fed me lies and continued my spiral of shame. I was desperate to feel accepted, so I allowed myself to get caught up in activities that were against my beliefs. I allowed myself to be taken advantage of, and I acted in ways that *I will always regret.*

But during that time, I also allowed myself to dream. I would imagine that I felt the weight of the world lift from my shoulders. I dreamed that I had the courage to declare that I belonged, and that my opinion was important and mattered. I envisioned those criticizing eyes turning to admiration, and I longed for a time when I wouldn't feel like I was screaming into the abyss.

Those moments were always short-lived. I'd realize there was no hope, and slip back into shame.

I'd like to say there was one thing that served as the catalyst to change it all for me. There wasn't. It was a series of mini-events that allowed me to crawl out of the depths of despair and move from short gasps of air to actually filling my lungs with purpose.

During my senior year, I had an epiphany of sorts. With high school ending, it was time to embrace new opportunities. I believed it was the only time I would be able to break free of the shackles holding me down. It was my last chance to find myself and be happy, then carefully remove the mask that I had lived with for so long.

I had no idea how I would do it. I didn't know if it was even possible. I had always been a bit scrappy, but I needed a lifeline to help pull me out of the dark hole.

Then, I met *him*. My now-husband, David. Even at only eighteen years old, I knew right away that he was my "person." He saw the woman who was buried deep within me when he looked in my eyes, and I saw comfort in his.

It was a rocky beginning, and our love story isn't a typical love story. Still, he believed in me. He knew I was meant for more. But I kept sabotaging our happiness, because I felt unworthy. I was unwilling to accept his love, because I couldn't imagine what actual love felt like. I didn't love myself, so how could he possibly love me?

Despite all this, our relationship began to heal the wounds that had been caused by my neglect, and to bring light to all the dark places where the negative words had scarred me. My shield began to soften, but learning to overcome self-hatred is a difficult journey. Rising above the lingering shame took many, many years of hard work, but over time, David helped me reassemble all the pieces that had never actually fit the right way.

Fast forward a decade, to when I started my entrepreneurial journey. It was the very first time I was honest with myself and understood exactly what *I* wanted. Not what I perceived *other* people wanted me to be, do, or have. That was the first time in my life when I declared my desires for myself, and felt a flood of passion course through my veins. It brought a cautious feeling of hope back into my life. It created a spark in me that had never been lit. My energy began to burn bright.

Don't get me wrong—I didn't just wake up one day and say, "Today, I am starting my own business." That was never a path I believed I could take. It was only the one I saw briefly when I allowed myself to dream about the impact I could have on this world.

Originally, I started this gig because we were in desperate financial straits. It was at a point in our life together when we had massive amounts of love but very, very limited funds. We lost our first home because we just couldn't afford it. We scraped by...but we were too proud. Too proud to let in our family and friends. They had no idea of the hardships we were going through—they probably still have no idea. The fact is that, when they read this, they will know. They will be able to look back and remember those times, and the idea of that frightens me.

We were too proud to tell the world we needed help. We were too proud because, on the outside, we had it all together. But when your husband loses his job of ten years, you scramble. My measly preschool director job wouldn't even come close to paying our expenses. So, there we were in a new city, in a new house, far away from the people we loved. I found myself wondering—what do I do next? Where can we go from here? David was working two new jobs and I was embracing—or trying to embrace—my new role as a stay-at-home-mom, which is arguably one of the toughest jobs in the world.

It was a time of nervousness and worry. So I leaned on my grittiness.

I researched how to utilize my natural skills and found an online business I could seamlessly build with zero dollars and my determination. It was hard at first—not the actual *work*, but the debilitating fear of being a fraud in this new role. I felt like I was walking the halls of middle school all over again—like I was wearing that damn mask once more, after so many years spent trying to shed it.

But this time, I wouldn't let my innate feelings of worthlessness take hold. This was something I had to push through because our family needed it. This *had* to work. My children were counting on me.

And *I* needed it. For me. So I took hold of my emotions and stomped them out.

My business became the ultimate savior. The wounds that were held together by old, ragged bandages began to heal, and I started to feel like the woman I was created to be. This business led me to meet other women who lit my soul on fire, and who believed in me—and not the masked version that was great at pretending, either. The quirky, odd, unique version of me. And when I decided to go all in and relentlessly be *me*, my journey took off and my business exploded. I knew I'd found my *thing*. A renewed passion for life filled me, and the excitement was invigorating. Not only did I uncover my true powers and gifts, but I was able to bless my family with more income than we'd ever made in our previous careers.

But as soon as I experienced some success, I began to feel like a fraud again. I was in a new space—the digital marketing world. A world filled with so many other amazing and accomplished women who had far more experience than I did. How could I possibly measure up against them? And the more successful and accomplished I felt, the more I questioned my abilities and knowledge.

Who am I to think I can do this?
Who am I to say I'm an expert?
Who am I to make this amount of money?

Who am I to think I'm worthy of success?

Who am I to believe I'm someone to be heard?

Those doubts and questions ricocheted through my mind, flooding me with negative thoughts:

I feel like a fake and a fraud.

I just got lucky—I'm not actually successful.

I must not let them see me fail.

I wanted to crawl into a hole and disappear. I was worried I'd be exposed; that the curtain would be pulled back, and the humiliating laughter of the world would begin—*just like middle school*. It was a paralyzing fear. It felt like the world was spinning out of control, and like everyone knew I was a big phony. The walls were closing in, and I was suffocating.

The anxiety and panic attacks became a daily occurrence—until one day, it was too much. I opened up to a friend, and she let me in on a secret:

This fear *wasn't exclusive to me.*

Relief washed over me as I was properly introduced to this thing that had consumed most of my life. It even had a name—the fear, the self-doubt, the crippling sense of worthlessness had a *name*.

Imposter syndrome.

This new revelation catapulted me toward discovering how to combat this never-ending fear. Instead of continuing to live at the intersection of brazen ambition and self-doubt, I took imperfect action. I made the conscious decision to leap forward and not to freeze. I decided to be okay with not having all the answers, with not being the expert, with not being perfect. I was going to move past the tears and questioning of my self-worth, and fully step into my power.

As women, we so often undervalue the very things that make us special and unique—the things that come easily to us, but not to others. It can be extremely hard to accept our uniqueness in a culture that overanalyzes everything in our media-focused world. We get so caught up in the curated squares and perfect words that we begin to discount our true assets. We allow "likes" and "followers" to define our self-worth and our abilities. It becomes easier and easier to feel unworthy of our success, especially when our social media feeds are full of other people who seem to be achieving more than we are. But everyone has demons to fight, and any person you might wish you could be is most likely struggling in other areas of life. And just because you believe you can't do that thing you've always wanted to do, doesn't mean you're right about it. I certainly wasn't right about it, and if you're battling those same fears, *you aren't right, either.*

Pushing past imposter syndrome is completely possible. It certainly has been for me, and it changed my entire life—my marriage, my relationships, everything. What I've learned is that in order to move past feeling like a fraud, you have to change the narrative you tell yourself. You have to become aware of your inner voice, and give yourself permission to excel and own your gifts. And every time doubt creeps in, you must combat the negative thoughts with powerful affirmations of self-belief. Something that often works for me is reminding myself of these three things:

I'm good enough. I'm smart enough. I bring value and knowledge to all of my relationships.

This affirmation is saved on my phone, my bathroom mirror, and my computer, so I can always remind myself that I am worthy.

Journaling was also a helpful exercise for me. Putting my inner dialogue down on paper allowed me to see my thoughts from a new perspective and analyze them logically. Once I realized I was telling myself a story that had no merit, I was able to rewrite and reframe my negative thinking. Instead, I could create empowering thoughts that motivated me and made me powerful. Changing my inner dialogue in this way took practice and a considerable amount of time. It involved making a distinction between feelings and facts, and understanding that my emotions are not always indicative of my reality.

Here's how I reframed my thoughts:

Instead of, "I don't belong here," I say, "I belong everywhere, always."

Instead of, "My opinion doesn't matter," I say, "The world needs my unique voice."

Instead of, "I am not enough," I say, "I am always enough, and my fear doesn't change that."

Instead of, "There's no way I can handle this," I say, "I've faced many challenges before, and I've conquered all of them."

Instead of, "I've been rejected! I'm worthless!" I say, "Missing this opportunity may turn out to be a fantastic thing for me."

Taking action doesn't have to be a giant leap—it can be just a baby step in the right direction. Instead of feeling as though we always need to prove our worth, it's important to remember that we all have to start somewhere. So, take a deep breath and refocus your attention on your success. Overcoming your feelings of unworthiness doesn't happen overnight—it's not a single action, and we all try and fail before we succeed. But changing your mindset and reframing your narrative allows the transformation to begin.

The truth is there will always be someone smarter than you, wiser than you, more successful than you…but there is only one YOU! And who you are sets you apart from everyone else.

It's a little bit of tough love, but it's the honest truth. And, for me, it's comforting. There's less pressure to meet the impossible standards that I put on myself, or to achieve the unattainable goals that I set and inevitably fail at. Instead of perpetually thinking I need to play catchup, I can celebrate where I'm at now, enjoy the things that I'm doing well, and challenge myself accordingly while still following my passion.

Because that thing called *perfection*…

The moment when you'll finally be good enough…

Waiting until you're ready…

Succeeding without years of practice, perseverance, and shit happening while you're trying…

None of it is real.

Making mistakes, falling, getting back up, dusting yourself off, learning, and moving forward is all there is. And in order to be successful, to be loved…you don't need to achieve anything. What you need to do is wake up to the fact that you're good enough right here, right now. Nobody's going to "find you out," because there's *nothing* to find out. You are *not* a fraud. You are amazing, and you are who you're meant to be.

And if you step into the fullness of who you are, what the world will see is more of your greatness. So trust yourself—you've got this.

Here's to the massive impact you'll have in this world.

About the author: Amy Edge is a former childhood educator turned impact-driven entrepreneur. She is an operations and project management expert for visionaries and change-makers in the online space.

She has honed her skills through certifications to become a partner with her clients as an operational leader and integrator within their businesses. This strategic partnership increases profits, empowers their teams, and scales their businesses with complete ease and without frustration.

She is the founder of The Rising Sisterhood movement, the book, and our community, the "Collective." Amy desires to curate a platform to celebrate, empower, and lift up our sisters as we navigate toward changing our narratives and stepping into our greatness.

You can find her latest project at www.amyedge.com or on Instagram at @heyamyedge.

Faith

by Jillian Bright

An entire untouched pizza lay on the table before me as I squinted out the floor-to-ceiling windows of the airport café, waiting for my flight. The midsummer sun glowed orange and pink through the clouds and reflected off the rain-slicked tarmac. Over the last ten months, I'd sat in dozens of airports all over the world, from Sri Lanka to Scandinavia and now South America. But on all those other flights, I'd been alone and diving deeper into my wild adventure.

This time, I was pregnant. And I was going home.

It's hard to say when this story really starts, because it wasn't in that airport. It was a lot earlier—years earlier, even. Much like the depression and anxiety that were about to plague me for the next three and a half years, there was no definitive beginning or ending. And I definitely didn't see a clear way out.

Six months before, I was in Italy and reconnecting with Nic, an Italian guy I'd dated a few years back when we both lived in Costa Rica. On our first night back together, we had dinner and then zoomed through the streets of Rome on his motorcycle. He took me to the Forum at 3:00 a.m. and kissed me under the ruins. You can't not fall in love (again) with someone after that—*I* couldn't, anyway.

Three weeks later, when it was time for him to fly back to where he was living in Argentina, he asked me to come stay with him for a few months after I wrapped up my year-long solo trip around the world. He was almost done with his degree, and I could write while he studied for his exams.

It sounded perfect, this plan to relax, reconnect, and pull together all my notes and stories after a year of travel. I was ready to slow down, settle in, and finally write my book.

Then, at the last bus stop, right before I crossed the border into Argentina, I was robbed.

They took my computer, hard drive, passport, wallet, camera, even my journal and notebooks. They took *everything*, except my clothes. My words, my memories, my identity. Irreplaceable notes and half-finished stories, two book manuscripts. Everything I'd worked so hard to create, to become...gone.

My initial reaction was to narrow my eyes and get down to business. There was no way I would let a couple of low-life thieves destroy what I had worked so hard to create. I'd rewrite everything I could, and better than before.

Then, a few weeks after the robbery, Nic and I sat down for dinner at a fancy Mendoza restaurant, to celebrate officially getting back together. We ordered a nice bottle of Malbec, empanadas, *mollejas*, and thick Argentine steaks to celebrate, but the wine tasted like Everclear and vinegar and the food made my stomach turn. I was so happy, and yet I couldn't touch a bite.

I'd been holding onto the hope that my period was late because of the stress of the robbery, but I couldn't deny the signs any longer. The next day, I took a pregnancy test, and not even ten seconds later, two bright pink lines glowed off the stick.

It was shock layered over shock. At first, I didn't feel anything. I just walked into the kitchen and told Nic it was positive.

As he sat there, staring at me in disbelief, I lit up a cigarette and looked out the window, over the concrete buildings and the city treetops to the Andes. The mountains I'd thought I was going to climb after I wrote my book. They were less than fifteen minutes from our apartment, yet they now seemed a lifetime away. It felt like everything I'd worked so hard for, everything I'd always wanted, had been yanked right out of my hands and replaced with this tiny thing that I didn't even want.

As feeling slowly trickled back into my being, the only emotion I felt was fierce, hot rage.

But if I was angry about the new life growing inside me, Nic was terrified—and for good reason. He wasn't done with school yet, and his parents were still supporting him financially until he graduated. I had just been robbed. Neither of us had jobs or a long-term place to live. It was hardly the most stable environment in which to usher a new human into the world. Since abortion is illegal in Argentina, I booked a flight back to California.

So there I was, in that airport, staring out the window as the sun sank into the Buenos Aires skyline, sipping fizzy water and trying not to puke or cry or scream when a thought occurred to me.

What if you just let yourself be happy about this?

As I let the question sink in, I became acutely aware of the fact that I actually *wanted* to be happy about this. I didn't want to be angry. I didn't want to get an abortion. And I didn't want to go back home.

I hadn't even realized I wanted a child, but here it was, and I suddenly really, really wanted it. Maybe it was too late to stay in Argentina, but it wasn't too late to change my mind about my baby.

***

My pregnancy didn't feel like real life. I felt like I was living in an alternate reality, where on any given day I could wake up, and my life would be back to normal. Except I didn't. I went from free-spirited adventurer and travel writer to broke and living with my parents in my small hometown. My partner was six thousand miles away, and if we wanted to stay together, I'd have to pick up and move back in with him just two months after our son was born.

My anger and sadness felt unmanageable, so I found a therapist who told me I was remarkably self-aware, and she wasn't sure why I was seeking therapy. I stopped going and started getting really worried about postpartum depression. Statistically, women who have unintended pregnancies are more likely to experience postpartum depression than women who planned to get pregnant, but there are lots of other factors that have the potential to affect any mother (or birthing person or partner, for that matter): teen pregnancy; depression before or during pregnancy; a family history of depression; stressful events such as illness, job loss, or a big move; rocky relationships; financial problems; difficulty breastfeeding; or a weak support system.

Aside from not being a teen mom and not knowing how breastfeeding would go yet, my situation checked all the boxes—especially if I chose to return to Nic in Argentina.

Even though I'd spent more time away than at home throughout the last fifteen years, the idea of packing up my tiny baby and leaving my family and friends behind broke my heart. But if it was a choice between staying where I felt I had support, or leaving in order to keep my new little family together…I would go, even if things between Nic and me were still fresh and uncertain.

However, instead of going back to chic Mendoza after our son was born, the three of us moved to Nic's parents' vineyard in the rural northwest, up in the high desert just east of the Atacama Desert. Our home-for-the-moment rested at the bottom of a sun-soaked desert valley in the foothills of the Andes, surrounded by nothing but towering cardon cactus and desert scrub. As far as the eye could see, there wasn't anything made by humans, save a splash of lights from the nearest town on the hillside at night.

I'd been a mom for just a few months at that point, and caring for my baby felt more natural than I ever knew it could. But I was utterly exhausted to the depths of my soul, and I felt like I'd lost myself forever. I wasn't able to recognize even a fragment of my life from before, and I would hold my son close, silently begging to find the joy in motherhood, feeling nothing.

On those hard days, our morning walks through the desert saved me. Out there, alone with my son and the hundred-year-old cacti that towered over us, the tiny ants that harvested the cactus flowers around our feet, the wild guinea pigs, the hawks, the condors…out there, with all that open space, there was finally room for everything I felt. The sun burned away the tears and the wind carried away the heaviness. In those early months, the desert felt like a womb, and I was slowly becoming.

I didn't fall in love with my son immediately. There was no wild rush of oxytocin when he was born, no immediate and overwhelming sense of rightness and perfection in this new life that I'd heard described by lots of new moms. My love for him grew in tiny pieces that took a long time to fit together, but I kept trusting that they would. I knew I wanted him. I knew I loved him, but I could still imagine my life without him. In fact, some days I yearned for it.

And so, out into the desert we walked. Every morning, with each footprint in the sand, I let go of another tiny piece of that life from before—a life that was now long gone.

***

After seven months in Argentina, we moved to Italy. A month later, I fell apart.

I hadn't seen my family or any of my friends for almost a year. There was no more wide-open desert to walk every morning. But there *was* a deep, lonely wedge in my relationship with Nic, and it was growing daily.

I cried uncontrollable, heaving, sobbing, desperate tears every day for five months. I had never felt so alone. I hated my life. I hated being a mom. I couldn't find joy anywhere, and I couldn't seem to let go of what I could never have again. The things I had so painstakingly developed my entire adult life were gone: my independence, my freedom, my sense of adventure, my sexuality, my confidence in myself, my faith in life and in the unknown that I had trusted when I allowed myself to feel happiness about my pregnancy.

I replayed the decisions I'd made more times than I can count. Why did I move in with Nic in Argentina when I was running out of money? Why did I keep a baby I wasn't ready for? Why did I leave my family to start a life with a man on the other side of the world? And why did I keep choosing to stay?

That's right—I *chose* this. *All* of this. So why wasn't I happy? What was I doing wrong? Did I just need to have faith that I was still in the darkness of the womb, and hadn't been born yet? Or that I was a butterfly growing wings, cramped up in this prison of a chrysalis? Maybe it just wasn't time yet, and I didn't know it. Maybe I didn't notice I was growing wings because I was too frantic to get out.

Was that it? Was I growing wings?

But what if I didn't want to fly? What if I wanted to put down roots? Worse, what if I wanted to do that in a world that didn't exist anymore?

I missed my family. I missed my friends. And, more than anything, I missed human touch. I didn't even know how long it had been since I got more than a brief, unfeeling hug from my partner. We hadn't had sex in over a year. Was that normal? Did it even matter what was normal? Could I still have postpartum depression a year after my child was born?

Yes, actually. The answer to that last question is that you absolutely can.

I sat down at my computer one day and searched "Help, I hate being a mom." I read post after post from women who said they hated their children. Women who said they didn't want kids, but did it to keep their partner or to make him happy. Women who were contemplating suicide.

It terrified me.

If I didn't pull myself together, was that where I was headed? Would this resentment I felt toward my tiny, innocent son start to sink into his subconscious? I had dated men whose mothers didn't love them enough. Controlling, jealous men whose inner child was so deeply wounded, they left a trail of abused women behind them.

No, I told myself. I would never let that happen to my son.

***

It took two years for me to recognize that I was dealing with postpartum depression and anxiety. I didn't want to admit it for a long time, because it was such a loaded admission, and things didn't look bad on the outside. I just felt lost and achingly alone.

I felt like I didn't have a right to be depressed. And yet, I was.

I'll be honest—I didn't know what to do. I didn't feel comfortable enough with my Italian to find a therapist in Italy, and I didn't have enough money to hire one without any insurance in the U.S. I didn't want to go on medication, but I was also afraid what might happen if I didn't. And, above all, I was really, really sick of feeling sad.

So, I took Leo back to California to visit my family for five months, just the two of us, and for the first time since he was born, I felt like I *had* made the right choice—that I *did* love being a mom, that there *was* joy in my choice. It was the first time I realized just how important having a strong community really is. A few months after we got back to Italy, I stopped breastfeeding, the hormones evened out, and the clouds lifted some more.

Then, in early 2020, my writing business started to take off, and I made my first friends in our little Italian town. I slowly began to feel like myself again, only stronger, more capable, and more compassionate. I still have days when I feel lost in the darkness, but my relationship with Nic has grown, and I have a small handful of new but supportive friends. When those moments find me, I call someone who makes me laugh or ask Nic for a really long hug, or I paint or write without caring how terrible it's going to turn out. And I know in my heart that it will pass.

Those words and photos that were stolen from me in Argentina are lost forever. I'll never get them back. But in spite of everything, I've found my voice again. I'm helping others find theirs through my writing and retreats. I wrote a children's book about our morning walks in the desert, and I even have a publisher for one of my books that was stolen—a memoir that is so much richer now than it ever would have been as a collection of travel stories.

The truth is, when you take a leap of faith, and trust your heart when everything else doesn't make sense, it's not the leaping that requires you to trust yourself the most. It's not even the freefall afterward. It's when you realize you can't actually fly—the crash landing of complete self-doubt where you can't move or even breathe because you're in so much pain, and you *know* you messed up and don't think you'll ever trust yourself again.

That's when you begin to understand that you have to grow your own wings. You can have faith in Life or in God, but if you don't have faith in yourself, too, you'll never get up. You'll never fly. Falling doesn't mean that you made a mistake. It means you had courage.

Don't let anything hold you back from knowing and following your heart. Take that leap of faith and own it—*live* it. And if you leap and find yourself alone in the darkness of crushing depression or self-doubt, have faith in yourself and reach out for help. We all go through challenging moments in our lives, but no one deserves to be stuck at the bottom forever. Finding your way out isn't easy or fun, but you *can* do it. Life is so much more beautiful on the other side.

About the author: Jillian Bright is an award-winning travel writer, author, copywriter, ghostwriter, retreat leader, and mama whose mission is to empower womxn, especially other moms, by telling stories, amplifying voices, and creating sacred space and community.

She believes that when we truly listen, connect, and collaborate, each of us contributing our unique voices, stories, and skill sets, we WILL create a better world for our kids and our future generations.

Jillian is currently working on a historical fantasy series set in the ancient Mediterranean and organizing retreats and adventures in Italy. *The Rising Sisterhood* is her second book as a contributing author, and her memoir, *The Trouble with Wings*, comes out June 15, 2021.

Jillian is originally from Northern California and now lives in the Italian countryside with her winemaker partner and their son. You can find her latest project at www.jillianbright.com or on Instagram at @wildbrightandfree.

Awakening

by Sharon White

I was born a pure, shiny, beautiful diamond wrapped in a big dose of anxiety and fear, thanks to my biological mother and her schizophrenia. (Not that I'm blaming her, as it is a terrible disease.) I used to think things like: What if I was born to a mother who could show me love? What if I was allowed the freedom to be myself? What if I was nurtured and encouraged? How would life be different? How would I act differently if I didn't have this anxiety? What if I felt supported? Am I going to be unbalanced like her? Why am I so weird? What if I didn't have to struggle to be "normal"?

Before I carry on, I want to say I have now realized there is no "normal," and that we are all unique. When I talk about "being normal," it's really the younger me talking.

In any case, I was never like the other kids, and had some quirky behaviors during my early years due to copying my mother's actions. I learned that our world shapes us most deeply from birth until the age of seven, and we also pick up emotions from our mothers while we're in the womb. My mother suffered anxiety due to her mental illness, which meant that I was similarly affected.

Unfortunately for my beautiful, big, shiny diamond, I had layers and layers of fear and anxiety wrapped around me. I was scared of being visible, because I associated being seen and heard with getting hurt. So I played small, and tried to blend in. I was scared of public speaking, so speaking out loud in a classroom never happened, as every time I knew I had to do this, I told my dad and stepmother I was sick and stayed at home. The mere thought of it would bring on panic attacks and a huge red rash across my face and chest—which, of course, made things a thousand times worse.

I couldn't look at my own eyes in the mirror. I was uncomfortable with eye contact in general, and the act of looking in the mirror made me feel like the devil was looking back at me. (Yes, that's a very quirky one.)

I didn't know how to interact with other children—I felt safer watching from a distance. Having this social anxiety didn't exactly make me many friends. I was alone, but I can't remember if I ever felt lonely, because I had heaps of imaginary friends to play with. I felt safe with them, which I'm sure made me fit in with the crowd.

Many of these behaviors followed me through my childhood, although my circumstances changed when dad remarried. Suddenly, I had brothers and sisters to play with. It took me a while to integrate and be "normal," but I did it! And after I had learned to interact and make friends, I realized I was pretty good at it. In fact, creating connections and building relationships became a superpower that I still use today.

I had overcome so many challenges from my childhood, yet anxiety was still a major part of my life. I needed to get rid of it.

I remember the day I busted through anxiety. I was in my thirties, and I had lived with it for so many years that it was an old friend by then. Until, one day, I realized it did not serve me. Anxiety itself was the one thing holding me back. It was controlling me. I don't like being controlled, and once I had this realization, I knew it was time to say goodbye.

I needed to eliminate this anxiety once and for all, so I challenged myself to become a teacher. I knew that teachers *have* to be seen and heard, and I saw how perfect this could be for overcoming my anxiety.

I had previously qualified as an NLP and hypnotherapy practitioner, so I knew how powerful the techniques were at creating change. I thought it would be perfect for me to take the next step and teach a subject that had helped change me so profoundly, so I began training to be a neuro-linguistic programming teacher.

This was how I eventually found myself standing on a stage in a theater in Sydney. I'd known this day was coming, and there was no way I could get out of it this time. I had to face my fear.

I was in a safe place. I was with my classmates, who had been going through the training with me. I had a wonderful teacher. *But,* I also had anxiety. Much more than ever before. It came flooding over me in uncontrollable waves, and I had no idea what to do.

The time came for me to speak. The moment I had been dreading had finally arrived.

I stood there, and no words came out.

I stood for more than ten minutes, and *nothing* except noises of pain: sobbing, wailing, and whimpering.

I wanted to curl up in a ball and hide. The feeling of fear was taking over my body. I couldn't think straight; I couldn't even move. It was as if time had stopped, and I was in hell. I felt tormented and worthless, fragile and powerless. My whole body was shaking, and inside, I wanted it all to be over. I felt like running off the stage, but I couldn't move.

I looked at my classmates, and I could see love and compassion in their eyes, but that didn't matter. For me, in that moment, I was completely overwhelmed with fear. Frozen. Stuck.

I stood there crying, shaking, and pleading with my eyes for my classmates and teacher to release me from my misery. I was sure my voice had disappeared, and I remember thinking—why am I putting myself through this? All the self-doubt from my childhood came flooding over me, and I felt like I wanted to die.

What made it worse was that the day before our assignment, our teacher had asked us to tell a metaphor on stage. But the only personal anecdote that came to my mind in that moment was the story about my dad dying. I have no idea why, but apparently my subconscious mind had a goal for me. It was telling me this was the perfect opportunity to release my fears. So, I guess a story about my dad dying felt like a great metaphor, as I stood there frozen and on the cusp of death.

Ten minutes of crying, snorting, shaking, and pleading felt like an eternity, but then it stopped. I was in complete terror and then…I stopped crying. I stopped shaking. I was able to open my eyes and look at the class, and my words were set free. The anxiety had burnt itself out!

My teacher looked at me and said, "Carry on. Tell your metaphor."

And I did. I was able to tell the story about my dad's death. I felt like a huge weight had been lifted off my shoulders. I had broken through my fear and recounted the worst story of my life at the same time. I felt an enormous sense of release.

When I finished, I received a round of applause from the class. Afterward, everyone individually approached me with a huge hug. I was giddy with relief—I'd faced my biggest fear, and while it wasn't elegant or ladylike, I did it, and I survived! The actual release of anxiety was exhausting—all the bottled energy from the last ten years finally spilling out of my body—but I also felt free.

That day was an amazing wakeup call for me. I can be visible. I have a voice, and some people are open to hearing what I have to say. Public speaking still isn't my favorite thing to do, but when I come off stage, I feel a natural high. I no longer have anxiety about being seen and heard, and I even run a YouTube channel about holistic health and help clients who are suffering from anxiety, depression, and emotional blocks. With practice, I am much more comfortable in front of the camera. I do live videos for my community and hold the space for others to heal, and I love it. I am confident in doing it.

Even though I suffered from anxiety—and in the moment, I thought I was going to die—it somehow made me feel alert and alive. When I was most anxious, it was about the things I wanted, and that means there was some passion driving me to succeed. So, I kept trying. And as you can imagine, anxiety over public speaking was not the only layer of shit I had to deal with. Looking at people, talking to people, being with people, and looking at myself made me anxious, too. These were other journeys I went on. Overcoming those layers takes effort and commitment, but it is so worth it once you're on the other side. Do it step by step. Layer by layer.

I spent years wishing I was different, wishing I was whole, wishing I was the same as everyone else. But eventually I realized that I am perfect just the way I am, and you are, too. Once *you* realize this, you will understand that the challenges you've faced in the past were invaluable lessons. Those lessons helped you survive and grow stronger, and now, you have everything you need within you to be everything you ever wanted. You just need to find your inner courage. You are the god of your own universe, and you can be whoever you want. You don't need permission from anyone else.

The hurdles I had to go through made me stronger in the areas that I needed to lead a community and help people heal. After all, how could I help others if I hadn't already done it for myself? There's no way I would be such a great therapist if I hadn't gone through this life just as it has played out. Everything happens perfectly, and for a reason.

It is important to embrace the whole of you, even though you may still have layers of shit to get through. We are all a work in progress, and we have already made a lot of progress. But some people want to hear your voice. Some people want to see you. Many people love who you are and can already see your potential, even though you may not right now. People who love you want to cheer you on and see you succeed. And even though you can do this on your own, it's great to do it with people supporting you.

Embrace your uniqueness. Be happy to be different from the norm. When you are comfortable with yourself, you naturally attract people like you, and when you love yourself, you will love the people you attract. Be okay with your layers of shit, and uncover it layer by layer. The secret is to do it one step at a time—don't try to change everything at once. Pick the one thing that you want to change in your life right now, and go for it. When you've mastered that, pick another thing and go for that, too.

Once you do this, you start feeling empowered, because you *know* you can overcome anything you want to. You *know* you can be and do anything you dream of doing and being. *You* have the power to create anything you want. And if there is something in your life that isn't working, it's down to you to make a change and make it work. Know that this is possible.

Now, that is a powerful realization. And once you are empowered, you can more easily follow your dreams, whatever they may be.

So, keep on your journey. Keep looking forward. Keep being authentically you.

You are a beautiful diamond. You are unique. And you have a powerful message.

Shine your light brightly, because you are perfect as you are right now.

About the author: Sharon is a therapist, coach, writer, and speaker who helps people live their dream lives, clearing emotions and beliefs that are holding them back so they can live their true purpose and passion. She has been in the health and wellness industry since 1996.

As a practitioner, she started her journey as a body therapist specializing in the disciplines of massage therapy, reflexology, reiki, and personal training. The desire to heal from the inside out inspired her to train in mind therapies and working with the subconscious mind.

She is a journey practitioner, master practitioner of hypnotherapy, and trainer of NLP, timeline, and matrix therapies. Integrating her approach and tailoring a therapeutic plan for each client gives her a unique understanding of their needs, which deliver long-lasting results.

You can find her latest project at www.globalhealingexchange.com/emotional-freedom-program or on Pinterest at www.pinterest.com.au/globalhealing/.

Unburdened

by Tonia Rolle Jones

Skin. It is less than a millimeter thick, yet it can determine everything people perceive about you.

Every day, I am forced to consider my skin. Whether I am peering at myself in the mirror, walking to my mailbox, or anywhere else—there is always a focus on my skin color. This chance of nature comes with a load of blessings and challenges, and I'm always amazed that something as random as your complexion can determine so much about your life, whether consciously or subconsciously.

I don't wake up every morning thinking about my complexion. Instead, I think about what I have to do for the day. I listen to the sounds of my children bustling around the house. I converse with my husband to confirm our schedules.

When I think about it, in many ways, my life is no different than most women. At least, in my head, I believe it is the same. I drive my children to school, meet friends for coffee, and run errands. I move through the days and the motions like most women. But there is always a lingering thought, always a silent scream, always a hindrance just out of reach.

My complexion. I am a brown-skinned American woman.

So, even though my routines are similar to those of others, they are etched with fear and worry. Worry about how my children, my husband, and I will be perceived and ultimately judged.

It starts with something as innocent as clothing. *What are my children wearing?* Most parents I know review what their children are wearing to school in order to meet the approval of dress codes. Instead, I am looking for any indication that my children and I are dressed in a way that would make us a target for racism, because every day, I am bombarded with videos of people who look like me being stopped by police or overly "concerned" citizens and harassed about *why we are in their neighborhood.* Which, in reality, is *our* neighborhood, too.

To help counteract this, I make a point of shopping where my Caucasian mom friends do, so that my children will look like they're part of the neighborhood, and their only difference is their complexion. This isn't something I began doing once my children started attending school—I was doing this from the day my son was born. I would always take him to nursery school in polo shirts—never T-shirts—because I wanted to project that he was a proper young man even as a toddler. Of course, I will concede that clothes won't change how people see me if they're determined to focus on my complexion, but I feel I have to *try*. I have to try to feel as if I can control the uncontrollable.

These are not "crazy" rationalizations. They are not ideations or irrational reactions. This is our reality, and I am afraid.

My concerns don't stop with our outward appearance and how we dress. These fears manifest in all areas of our day-to-day life, even with a task as straightforward as driving. Before I ever move my car out of the driveway, I ensure that all my lights are working and my state inspection sticker is up to date. And once I begin my drive to work or to run errands, it's imperative that I am always a very cautious and considerate driver. After all, I don't want to have a reason to be stopped by any law enforcement officers.

Let me explain.

I am not a smuggler or a felon. I am simply a brown-complexioned American woman driving a car. It may sound innocent or overly cautious to be concerned about the simple act of driving a car around town, but I know the names of too many people who didn't survive their routine traffic stops for lane changes or blown tail lights.

People who look like me.

I make a point of speaking to all the police officers I see in my neighborhood, in the hopes that if I am ever pulled over, they will remember my face. Many of these encounters were very professional, with incredibly kind officers.

I have also had officer encounters where I was yelled at and unreasonably detained, but I am thankful that I was able to drive away.

It's a shame that the country I love and adore has a love-hate relationship with the color of my skin. Athletes and entertainers can enjoy boundless love and attention from the masses—until they speak out about the ills or injustices in our society. Just look at the many examples of these backlashes: Tommie Smith and John Carlos, perhaps. Or maybe you're more familiar with Colin Kapernick?

Politicians aren't safe from this love-hate relationship, either. President Donald J. Trump told sitting Congresswomen who were of African descent to go and run their *own* country when they criticized him. And it wasn't because they were members of a different political party—he was also very critical of a fellow party member who was of African descent.

A person's complexion is powerful in our society. It's intriguing that the founders of our country picked such a random characteristic as skin color to serve as the basis for segregation and judgement. My best assumption is that skin color is a quick and easy identifier, but I am curious—if we all shared the same skin color, would we have assigned supremacy or dominance to the height of a person? Or some other characteristic?

The saddest aspect of our society as it relates to skin is in our use of the word "race." We are all human—there is only one race. There are multiple ethnicities, yes, but when we as a society accept that our skin color somehow makes us a different race, we are able to devalue each other with stereotypes and laws.

During the summer of 2020, we were forced to take a look at our skin and the division within our nation. Many Americans were brought out into the streets in protest over the brutal killings of other Americans—Americans who were my complexion. The circumstances of their murders and their treatment was a shock to many people, but it was not a shock to me. I have seen this before. I have been a witness to this brutality for many years. The pain is all too familiar, and overwhelmingly heartbreaking each time.

There are many books, movies, articles, and monuments documenting the mistreatment and violence against people with a different skin color—*my* skin color. But I don't want you to think that the color of my skin is a self-imposed (or, rather, society-imposed) limitation that rules my life. It does not. I enjoy the skin I am in. But our country is a place of great diversity and opportunity, and I want to gently challenge you to examine your surroundings.

Do you interact with people who are different from you in any way?
Do they look different?
Do they worship differently from you?
Do they have different ancestors than you?

Building a wall of empathy and allyship is imperative to bridge the divide of our society. Being an ally—a person who is not a member of a particular marginalized group, but seeks to help end the oppression of those in the marginalized group—is a constant process. Allyship can mean different things to different people, and it can be tough to know where to begin.

The first step is to *start*. Educate yourself, ask questions, be vulnerable. Stand up for the wronged, use your voice to support and empower others, stand in solidarity. Allyship is a process, and along the way, you're sure to do or say the wrong thing now and then. Don't get defensive. Take responsibility for your slip-ups, and do better moving forward.

In my everyday life, I have no other option but to engage outside of my comfort zone. However, I make it a personal goal to learn more about people and their lives during these interactions, and I hope you will, too. This is not a plea for political correctness—it is a request that you expand your knowledge of who Americans really are. And I know from experience that challenging yourself to engage in a new experience will not only make you richer in your spirit—it will enhance your empathy.

About the author: Tonia Rolle Jones is a passionate and fiercely loving person, demonstrated by her actions, causes, and activities.

Tonia obtained her bachelor's degree from the University of Richmond in Virginia, majoring in speech communication and minoring in women's studies. She used her degree and skills working for Fortune 500 companies in management positions.

She decided to leave the corporate world in 2015 to open her own business with her husband and life partner, Scott Jones. Together they successfully launched and operated Jones Ventures, LLC, which was publicly known as Chef on the Go and The Chili Wagon. Tonia managed the marketing and day-to-day operations of both companies until a catastrophic illness hospitalized her off and on for the better part of 2017. She continues to battle the illness, but decided in 2019 to launch Mommy Taxi, a transportation service for unaccompanied minors, after seeing the need to assist single working moms with transporting their children.

You can find her latest project at www.facebook.com/TWXmommytaxi or on Instagram at @toniarollejones.

Section 2

Giving Yourself Permission to Step into Your Power

"If you want to achieve greatness, stop asking for permission."

—Brian Tracy

Are you constantly refraining from standing up, from speaking out, from living your truth? Women so often are the martyrs—the person who puts everyone else's needs first. The one who always eats last. The caretaker of the family. The leader putting in all the overtime needed to grow a business.

Other times, the trauma from our childhood seeps into our present, which subsequently causes us to mute ourselves. We hold ourselves back. We tiptoe. We don't actively reach for more. We don't demand ownership of our power.

To be in your power is to claim your joy, deliver your gifts, and own your part in the life you create. So, give yourself permission to live a big life. Step into who you are meant to be. Stop playing small. Realize that, no matter the circumstances, you have the power to choose, to prioritize your best interests, and to ultimately create the life you really want to live.

You're meant for greater things.

Fighter

by Kayleigh Hanlin

Society defines a "fighter" as someone who displays strength, whether that be mentally, emotionally, or physically. A fighter is someone who overcomes the worst obstacles of her life and still comes out on top; who doesn't let the naysayers stop her from accomplishing her dreams.

Most days, I am still trying to figure out if I would call myself a fighter. How can I be a fighter when I tend to break down in the face of the simplest criticisms? Why would anyone label me as a fighter when I'm always so angry with the "powers that be" for the health issues I've had to face? And don't get me started on how many things in life I have quit because of someone else's opinion.

According to society's standards, that is not what a fighter looks like. *That* is not how a fighter is supposed to act. And yet a "fighter" is what I've often been called by family members, friends, and even strangers. If so many believe I'm a fighter, then I suppose it must be true, regardless of how I see myself.

I have a hard time accepting a compliment—perhaps you do, too—but what I can accept as truth is this: I have a hidden strength that seems to appear when I least expect it. Something deep within me takes over, and I become a new person. When I am struggling to move forward, or bogged down in a state of negativity, this new person digs out that hidden talent and takes over. It brings the confidence I didn't know I had up to the surface. It tells the negative self-talk to mind its own business. It moves me from darkness into the light, and because of all this, I begin to believe in myself.

I believe this hidden talent was developed during my childhood. On day one, to be exact. Full disclosure, though: It took me many years, along a very bumpy path of evaluating my belief system, before I was able to embrace and understand this talent. So, in order to share my full journey, let's start from the beginning.

On the day of my birth, my mom endured twelve hours of labor with my heart rate soaring and dropping like an eagle in flight. This was a clear indication that something was off. When I finally appeared in the world, my skin was bluish-grey, and my little body was lifeless, my lips devoid of that telltale newborn wail. The medical staff immediately jumped into action, so fixated on figuring out what was wrong that they completely forgot to show my parents their new baby before rushing me out of the room.

Within a few hours, the doctors diagnosed me with a heart defect, but they knew that I needed more treatment and care than their local hospital could handle. Still, it was three weeks before I was stable enough for the doctor to sign off on an ambulance ride to a better equipped hospital in Cleveland, an hour's drive away from my hometown. Needless to say, that was a very tense ambulance ride for my parents.

At the new hospital, I was diagnosed with two congenital heart defects: tricuspid atresia and ventricular septal defect. In layman's terms, these conditions rendered the right side of my heart useless, and the rest of my heart was making up for it by redirecting the blood flow elsewhere. The doctors were direct with my parents when providing the prognosis, telling them their firstborn child might not live—that they should prepare for the worst.

Now, I don't know about your family, but my big, loud, Irish-Italian relatives didn't just roll over and give up when they heard this news. Instead, my parents and extended family tried everything they could to keep my (and frankly their own) spirits up. The goal was to stay positive as I underwent *three* open-heart surgeries. My parents had been exposed to the power of positive thinking way before it was "the thing," and they believed that to get through these surgeries, we needed to recognize the positive experiences along the way and focus on the goal of getting me healthy enough to return home.

Thus began the years of doctor visits, surgeries, and poking and prodding that made me feel like a ragdoll being tossed around from person to person. My family prayed—a *lot*. They went to church and asked others to pray for me. They made sure the nursing staff didn't miss me on the rotation when passing the TV cart from one room to the next with the only movie the hospital had (*The Wizard of Oz*). They bribed me with Twizzlers during the endless rounds of bloodwork, IV inserts, and catheters. But most importantly, my parents never gave up. They never stopped believing that I would grow stronger—and neither did my younger self.

Due to the extensive amount of time I spent in a hospital bed, I didn't have the opportunity to learn to crawl, stand up on my own, or walk in the same manner as my peers. I had to undergo physical therapy in order to learn how to use my legs to get around. Up until then, getting from one point to another had involved either someone carrying me or scooting on my butt while pushing myself with my hands. I was nearly two-and-a-half years old before I was finally able to walk on my own. Even so, I was a force to be reckoned with. This girl did it all—perhaps a bit dramatically, but I got through three open-heart surgeries successfully, proving to the medical staff and everyone else around me that I was a fighter.

Until it was time to leave the hospital, that is. Because once I entered the real world, I quickly realized that I was not, in fact, a fighter.

I was a quitter.

***

At six years old, I was enrolled in dance class. I loved to dance anytime, anywhere, music or not. But once I was inside that studio with no one I knew around, I lost it. While I cried hysterically, my mom apologized and took me out of class. She swore never to return. That was fine with me, because I had no intention of returning. I was quitting and satisfied with my decision. Around the same time, my parents also signed me up for community soccer. That lasted only a few short weeks before I lost my glasses (and my mind) on the field. At that point, we all decided I wasn't yet ready to join my peers in group activities.

But then, one day, I was told that I *couldn't*. Someone who knew hardly anything about me told me that I wasn't capable of doing something every other kid around me was doing.

As I try to recall that moment now, my memories start to jumble. I can no longer recite the exact conversation, but I do vividly remember the feelings that bubbled up inside of me. There was a new physical education teacher at our school that year, and we were getting ready, as on many days before, to play a game in which there would be physical contact. The new teacher pulled me aside and told me this game was "too physical" for *someone like me*.

I had no idea what to do. That burning sensation in the back of my throat started, and my eyes welled up with tears. But instead of standing up for myself, I nodded my head like the good girl I was and obediently retreated to the sidelines, as the teacher ordered. When I sat down, I felt ashamed, confused, and hurt. I felt I had done something wrong, and that I was being punished for it by not being allowed to play with my friends. I couldn't do something that I had done previously, and I was at a loss as to the reason why.

It was at this moment that the kids in my class noticed something different about me. They were playing the game, but I was not. Logic told them something was off, and I was deemed *different*.

While my classmates learned I was not like them, I began to see that adults will often place labels on someone they have little information about—like when they learn I have a medical condition and have been through multiple surgeries. On hearing this news, most adults, consciously or not, suddenly saw me as breakable, fragile— someone who needed constant supervision. They immediately told me what I could and could not do based on their own sets of beliefs and experiences. They never gave me a shot. They just assumed I "couldn't" because of one piece of information. They didn't consider who I was as a whole person.

At an early age, I had to learn to push myself past the boundaries others set for me. Fortunately, I had wonderful parents who taught me very early in life that I know my body best. I was told many times to speak up when I felt funny or off, as that could be a sign of an issue (or perhaps not). Either way, whenever I spoke up about something not feeling right, I worked with an adult or trusted peer on how to assess the situation and resolve the issue. Speaking up for myself and my body also taught me that I needed to try before I said no.

Now, as an adult, I can empathize with where they were coming from. When looking after another person's child without the full knowledge of that child's life experiences up to this point, an adult will make assumptions based on what they feel is best. What I should have done that day was to show the teacher I was capable, but like most kids, I'd been taught to obey authority figures. However, as I got older, I realized something magical. I didn't enjoy it when people made assumptions about me or anyone else, regardless of their ability. I am perfectly capable of many, many things. And when I began to show others what I could do, it revealed a whole new side of me and gave me confidence in my abilities.

That is why I consider myself a fighter—because I learned how to trust myself.

***

Remember when I quit dance? Well, a few years later, in middle school, I decided to try again. Why? Because I really do love to dance, and I figured out that the reason I quit was because I was afraid to step outside the boundaries placed around me—by *me*. Not by others. That first dance teacher didn't tell me no—I didn't even give her a chance to. Instead, I constructed a belief in my mind that went something like this: "All those other kids don't have scars on their chests or seem out of breath after a few minutes, so I must not belong. I must be different, and therefore I can't do this."

I created my own frickin' boundary, and I wouldn't let myself cross it because of a limiting belief.

And so, as I went through middle school, I started to show others exactly what I was capable of. In addition to dance, I joined the basketball and volleyball teams and participated in all the practices and games, just like my teammates. During those critical growing stages, I pushed myself to match my peers, and it taught me the value of teamwork, how to handle competition, and the importance of learning a skill correctly. Those awkward years of middle school also taught me that I am *not* an athlete—I mean, standing at less than five feet tall during that time, I was pretty confident that basketball wasn't going to be my "thing, "but I still wanted to try and learn. I wanted to participate. I wanted to have the opportunity to enjoy all the same activities as my peers.

Looking back on what I endured, I'm impressed with my younger self for two reasons. First, for not letting anyone—especially someone "authoritative"—stop me from pursuing the activities I was passionate about. Instead, I trusted myself to listen to my inner voice and draw my own limits. Second, I was proud of myself for understanding that I *had* set my own limits, and that I needed to question those limits in order to move forward. I have since moved past the personality of a quitter and taken on the mindset of a fighter. I'll be honest—it took me years to really start fighting back against those limiting beliefs created by society and the community around me.

But when I finally figured out that I *could* fight…it was such a liberating feeling.

Mindset work takes practice. Questioning the limits and labels you have in your head, as well as the comments you hear from others each and every day, is difficult. But I believe we can all become better at setting our own limits by asking a few simple questions, like, "Who is this coming from?" and "Does this align with who I am?" By working through these questions, you will begin to backtrack and learn how you came to believe in them. Finding the source and then asking, "Is this even true?" will help you break free from the beliefs that are holding you back.

The final step is the best part. You now get to create your own, new belief around that idea, label, memory, or whatever it may be that you once held as truth. You get to shape your belief system, and that, my friend, is a powerful thing.

***

At the beginning of this conversation, I told you my perception of a fighter: someone who is strong in all aspects of life, overcomes obstacles, and doesn't let other people's opinions dictate her life. Take special note of that word: *perception*. Those qualities were what I thought a fighter should look like based on years in the American education system and absorbing societal norms. But, as we have learned, it's long past time to question what society, or the media, or your neighbor says about something. It's time to decide for ourselves what a fighter looks like.

Maybe to you, a fighter is a single mom who loves her kids and does what she can for them. Or it's the local businesswoman and her family, who have passed down their tradition of hard work from one generation to the next. Or maybe that fighter is *you*. Maybe *you* are the best example of a fighter anyone has ever laid eyes on. *You* get to decide what that word means and how it will impact your life—no one else.

So, while my day one was chaotic, the past eleven thousand or so days have also been a roller-coaster ride of discoveries and emotional experiences. I will continue to be the best example of a fighter for myself for as long as I am walking on this beautiful planet—and I hope you will be a fighter for yourself, too.

About the author: Kayleigh Hanlin is the co-founder of Empowered Minds and co-author of *J.O.Y Journal*. The *J.O.Y. Journal* is a guided activity journal for girls that takes the reader through creative prompts to help them discover and embrace their uniqueness while building self-love, confidence, and resiliency.

Kayleigh graduated with honors from Otterbein University with a bachelor of arts in public relations. She works in both marketing and project management in the publishing industry. Kayleigh serves as a board member for the Young Alumni Council for Otterbein University and Epsilon Kappa Tau sorority.

Kayleigh is a volunteer with the Make-A-Wish Foundation. She is an avid reader and enjoys exploring her local food scene and spending time with her family. Kayleigh resides in Columbus, Ohio.

You can find her latest project at www.mindsempowered.com.

Confidence

by Rachel Smets

Hola, hablo un poco español.

That's all I could say when I first landed in Spain twenty years ago and began my journey abroad. Since that moment, I have lived in many different countries, facing a wide variety of challenges and confronting complex fears, but back then, I was a woman alone, having to deal with the entire hassle of moving, visa paperwork, finding a job, learning a new language, and let's not forget the many, *many* times I got lost. Still, despite everything, that very first adventure to Spain was the start of an unforgettable journey to discover my purpose—and to find the confidence to inspire others.

At the age of twenty-four, I became fascinated by the idea of living abroad. I had little to no travel experience, since my parents really didn't care for traveling or elaborate vacations. They're the kind of people who love staying in their same home, same neighborhood, and same town, day after day, week after week, year after year. In other words, they love being in their comfort zone. However, I was in contact with expats on a daily basis through my work, and I liked the idea of moving to a new country—it sounded so magical and intriguing. At the time, I didn't think about cultural differences or how it would affect me, because every thought I had was nothing but glamorous. There was the trifling concern of possibly needing to learn a new language, of course, but since I already spoke four languages fluently, adding a fifth or sixth to my repertoire was the least of my worries.

Most people I knew thought moving abroad would be the biggest mistake of my life. My family and friends couldn't imagine why I would want to leap into the unknown and abandon my successful career, financial security, and everything I'd worked so hard to achieve. They wanted to keep me safe in their comfort bubble, and the thought of living in another country was, from their perspective, a huge risk, dangerous, unsafe, and completely irrational. I was devastated, torn between pursuing my dreams and heeding my parents' advice. Their opinions were loud and clear, and I knew if I went, I wouldn't be able to count on their support.

Facing a mountain of questions and doubt, I felt completely abandoned and on my own. What should I do? Who should I listen to—my gut, or my rational, roaring voice?

Despite the reservations of nearly everyone around me, there was one thing I kept thinking about: the pain of regret. When I was old and grey someday far in the future, I didn't want to look back at my life and wonder, "If only I had done it…"

Finally, I decided—I was determined to move abroad. Time for action! First, I broke down my big goal into small steps, which started by talking to more expats and asking them a ton of questions. Then, I began applying for jobs pretty much everywhere around the world. Of course, I could have saved some time by narrowing my search to just a few countries, but once I'd committed to the idea of going, I was eager to hit the ground running and find something as soon as possible. I was disappointed that I couldn't include my family in the planning process, since they weren't seeing any positives in the entire "abroad" idea, but I hoped they'd come around once they saw how well-prepared I was.

Finally, after months of applying, I was offered a job in Spain. I wound up living there for two years, kicking off a journey that would eventually see me living in fourteen different countries (and counting!). Spanish rapidly became my fifth fluent language, and I've added a couple more languages since then. Each time I moved to a new place, I took the time to research properly, find out what paperwork I needed, apply for jobs, and look for housing. Then, once I arrived, I had to adapt to *the new*—learning a new language, meeting new people, and finding my way around—so I could feel at *home*.

Being alone in so many new countries, away from everyone I knew, I had my share of days when tears came quicker than laughter. Many times, I found myself on my knees in an empty living room, surrounded by moving boxes, feeling exhausted and alone and desperately missing my mom. Thanks to technology, it's easy enough to keep in touch, but a phone call just isn't the same when you feel stressed or sad, and all you want is a hug. In those moments, loneliness would creep in, and that inner critic would ask why I'd moved, and if I'd made the right decision. What if I failed and needed to return to my family, who never wanted me to leave in the first place? What would they say? Could I handle everyone telling me, "We told you so"?

As the years passed, I realized that nobody is happy and joyful every single day, and I had to stop expecting all of my days abroad to be perfect. In other words, my happiness wasn't contingent on my choice of location, despite what my younger self might have believed.

Moving also became easier each time I did it, but even more importantly, I began to feel "at home" more quickly in each place, because I knew exactly how to create a routine, fill my days, and make friends. It was easier to connect with people in some countries than others, and my journey has definitely been scary at some points, but I keep reminding myself *why* I decided to do this in the first place: I wanted to meet new people and understand their cultures. And I never would have been able to do that if I'd remained in my hometown, as my parents wanted me to!

    I also learned that real fear is bred from our own negative thoughts. So often, I stressed myself by thinking, "I can't do it. I'm not good enough." What you say to yourself affects how you feel and also the decisions that you make. Slowly, I learned to be aware of my own negative thoughts, and how to shift them in a positive direction and create new, optimistic thoughts instead. Daily mindfulness was key to my transformation—being in the present instead of dwelling on the past or worrying about the future reduced my stress significantly. These practices made me feel so much more confident and allowed me to find opportunities instead of challenges. Each time I did something new and faced my fears, it always felt like climbing the highest mountain. But after that first climb, the mountain slowly became a hill, and climbing a hill is a fun hike.

    One simple example is when I was living in France, where I had just landed a job as a commercial manager, selling building materials. There I was, a foreigner with a strange accent, a woman in a male-dominated field, and—to make matters worse—I had never done this kind of job before. Can you imagine my anxiety? I could feel my heart beating in my throat before entering the front door of that huge building on my first day. But then I summoned my courage, knocked, entered, and with a polite *Bonjour*, started my speech. A few minutes in, I realized that despite all the obstacles before me, *I could do this.*

Victories like that definitely boosted my self-confidence.

My journey has also deepened my understanding of true friendship. Throughout my travels, I began asking myself: *Who are the people who really support me unconditionally? Who are the people I really want to be surrounded by?* I realized that the friends who genuinely care are the ones who understand that living abroad is an intense experience, rather than a holiday, and friendship isn't about the number of emails or calls—it's about being there for each other, no matter what, even if you haven't called or messaged them weekly.

During my years abroad, I have learned so much about people. Every time I arrive in a new country, I have to rely on strangers to help me learn my way around. And after so many conversations with new people, I've found that those who quickly tell me how wonderful and everlasting our new friendship will surely be are usually the ones I never hear from again after I've moved out of the country. Disappointment in those so-called friends has taught me to choose my circle carefully. Sometimes, this means letting go of the people who are pulling me down and draining my energy, which can be tremendously difficult. It also takes a while, but being surrounded by supportive people provides you with energy that motivates and inspires you!

That support is essential when you move abroad alone, rather than as a couple or a family. Being single seems easy for some people, and I often hear, "Oh, you're free to do anything you want!" True, but it also means I'm the only one making decisions. Which job, which house, which location, which insurance, which car, which gym, etc. Sometimes I would have appreciated sharing decisions and chores (or maybe I wouldn't have taken on that one job that turned out to be a disaster).

Good and bad decisions are both great life lessons and experiences. In fact, I love to use this saying in my speeches: "I never make the same mistake twice—I make them five or six times, just to make sure." I encourage everyone to make mistakes, because it helps you grow and develop yourself. When you do nothing, you can't fail, but you also can't learn and grow if you don't try.

Years ago, I never thought about my past mistakes in a positive light. Now, I understand failure is life's greatest teacher. Every "down" moment has an "up," and I keep moving forward. Each mistake is an opportunity to do things differently and make better choices.

Life has not always been easy. I've lost friendships, went through a divorce, and suffered burnout. I took on jobs that seemed amazing, but ended up being a disaster. Sometimes people say that I am so *lucky*, because I'm an independent woman, traveling the world, living in many countries, working as an international speaker and author, growing on YouTube, and achieving a freedom lifestyle.

Lucky? NO! I *created* this lifestyle—I followed my dream and worked damn hard to be able to do what I love, what I want, and what I desire. Now, I am proof it's possible, and I can help others create the life they desire, and change from doing what's *expected* of them to doing what they're truly meant to do.

My purpose is crystal clear: Help people to become their best selves! Or, more specifically, help people create an escape plan to transition from their 9–5 to a life of freedom and being their own boss, just like I achieved when I quit corporate to live this lifestyle. My goal is to motivate and inspire ambitious people, so they can make plans and take actions toward their goals, happiness, and freedom.

Happiness, success, and confidence are things I constantly work hard to achieve. The definition of those things is different for everyone; it's personal, and an inner feeling within ourselves. That's why I enjoy coaching and inspiring people online—it brings me pure joy to see people shine when they learn to believe in themselves and realize they can achieve their dreams.

In my journey, I have found that growth takes time and patience. You can start changing your life from feeling stuck to finding your own life path. This is the message I bring to my audience and readers, hoping it will move you to take charge of your life.

Are you ready to begin your journey? Then do it! "Life changes, and so can YOU!"

Start NOW!

About the author: Rachel Smets is a clarity coach, 2x TEDx speaker, author, YouTuber, and online course creator. Rachel helps mid-career professionals create a plan to escape their 9–5 and become an online entrepreneur with more freedom and time.

Rachel quit her corporate job at forty to have more freedom to travel the world and grow her income online. She now empowers her clients to find clarity, build confidence, and take actionable steps to turn their passion into income.

Rachel's bestseller, *Awaken Your Confidence*, explains how you can build confidence step by step, and her book *Living Abroad Successfully* is a practical guide to planning and enjoying a successful life abroad.

You can find her latest project at www.rachelsmets.com or on Instagram at @rachelsmets.

Decisions

by Giselle Grant

When I was nine years old, my mom made a living by selling clothes door-to-door. Most mornings, she would fill two enormous bags with kids' and ladies' clothing, then a third, smaller bag for me to carry. Since Mom didn't own a car, we would start our days bright and early and arrive back home in the afternoon, just in time for me to leave for school. We walked for miles, going up and down steep hills, walking on narrow, dirty streets filled with potholes and no sidewalks.

It was your typical suburb in a third-world country. Sometimes a stray dog would chase after us, or we'd wind up in the path of barefoot, shirtless kids playing soccer in the streets. We rang doorbells, knocked on tall iron gates, and walked past clotheslines, peeking our heads directly inside the open doors of countless humble houses. Each one had a unique shape and size, and most were still under construction, with exposed brick and unpainted walls on the inside.

I didn't understand why Mom would take me with her—surely all I did was slow her down. Hot sand and little rocks would creep into my flipflops, hurting my little toes, and my bag always seemed to get heavier with each step, no matter how much clothing we sold. We'd knock on dozens of doors and hear "no" over and over again, until I began to wish nobody would ever buy anything, so that Mom would give up the door-to-door hunt for clients. Other times, I was so tired and thirsty that all I wanted was for someone to say, "Yes, let me look at them!" so I could sit down for a moment.

The reality was my dad's salary barely covered food, and Mom didn't have an education. She would buy clothes from discounted retail stores and then resell them door-to-door. To make her wares more attractive to prospective buyers, she would ask for no upfront money down. People sometimes cheated and refused to pay her when the bill came due, but this tough reselling business was her only shot at overcoming the eternal lack of money in our household.

As a child, I didn't give a damn about her reasons—I just thought it was unfair that I had to spend hours walking on those dirt roads instead of watching television or playing with my dolls. I would sit down on the side of the street and throw a fit, tears of pain and frustration streaming down my face. I remember refusing to move any further, complaining that my bag was too heavy, that my back and hands hurt, or that the sun was giving me a headache.

Mom's response to this kind of behavior was very tough and direct. She always spoke to me as if I was an adult, and she would never get on the floor to hug me or explain anything in a kind or patient way. Instead, when I refused to cooperate, I'd hear loud and clear: "GET UP RIGHT NOW! Do you want to eat tonight? Get up! Pick up that bag, wipe those tears away, and thank God you have legs to walk and hands to carry!"

She would go on and on about how we had to sell clothes to keep the lights on or be able to afford other *superfluous* things, like yogurt. And if I didn't budge, she would offer me strong "incentives" (in the form of consequences) to help me get moving.

By today's standards, perhaps my mom didn't employ the most conventional or "acceptable" parenting methods. Some may even accuse her of practicing child labor. But I know now that Mom was doing the best she could. For that I'm thankful, and I love her deeply. Thanks to her, I have a warrior spirit. I know at times I'll get knocked down, but it's never okay to stay there. My past or present doesn't have to define my future, because my future will be what I *decide* it to be.

I decided early on that I wasn't going to have the same life as my mom. I literally hated the door-to-door selling, so I kept asking her, "What do people who have money do?" and "How does someone get rich?"

She would say she didn't know, but she thought it came down to education: "If you don't study, you'll never get a good job." She believed a good job at a big company was the way to make a good living. I was puzzled by that, because Dad went to high school and had a job, yet we were still poor!

With no role models, books, or Google to ask, I resolved to become a straight-A student. If studying was all it took to be successful, and success meant not having to knock on doors, I'd make it happen! So, when I reached middle school, I applied for an IT and data programming hybrid high school/associate's program. The only problem was that the school was hours away from my house. To be in class by 8:00 a.m., I had to also *decide* it was worth dragging myself to the public bus stop at 5:00 a.m. each day.

For three years, I averaged five to six hours of daily commuting on crowded public buses. I left my house before the sun rose at 4:40 a.m., stayed at the school until 5:00 p.m., and was back home after sunset, around 8:00 in the evening. It was exhausting, and there was no shortage of adult commuters who wondered why a thirteen-year-old girl was squeezing in among them. Several people tried to discourage me, voicing strong opinions about how I was wasting my time, but I was determined to prove them wrong.

I specifically remember one middle-aged woman with dark circles under her eyes and liberal streaks of white in her hair. She told me, "Educated people are scrubbing toilets nowadays, you better go back to sleep!"

The woman gave me a bitter look and met my defiant eyes as I thought, *Maybe if you had done something other than sleeping, you would not be stuck here like a sardine in this can right now!*

She had a seat and I was standing, so our faces were at the same level. Her words had just punched me in the stomach, and the muggy air mixed with other people's body odor made me feel sick. I opened my mouth to speak my thoughts—

"Giselle, you better respect the elders!"

My mom wasn't on the bus, but her voice echoed strongly in my mind before I had a chance to say anything. I nodded slowly, breathed in that hot air, and shut my mouth. Instead of delivering a sharp retort, I looked away, gazing outside the foggy bus windows. The traffic was especially bad that morning, and I knew I would probably be late for my coding class, but I was confident that this path was my only shot at having a different life. Why couldn't these other people see it?

***

The decision to attend that school indeed changed my whole life. I was the first person in my extended family to not only pursue secondary education, but also attend some of the best universities on the planet, where I graduated with honors.

Shortly after graduating from the University of Sao Paulo, I applied and was accepted for my dream job at a multinational corporation. I took part in a European leadership trainee program, and just a couple of years after leaving Brazil, I was receiving international awards for some of the innovative projects I led as a European marketing manager. My career gave me an amazing life I could have never dreamt of as a child, and that includes meeting my husband on a flight between Paris and Lisbon.

From an outside perspective, what you see is that I got married, had two beautiful sons, and founded a successful company that allowed me to work from home while enjoying my kids growing up. It sounds beautiful, doesn't it? But there's far more to it. While everything you see from the outside is true, I didn't simply "manifest" this perfect life from nothing. It's not some sort of laptop-lifestyle fairy tale that earns me money while I sleep. No—I worked my butt off to get here, and still do.

The decision to start my own company was rooted in struggle—and a particularly rough start to my marriage. At the time, I was working in Japan, but when my work assignment ended, I was supposed to return to my regional role in Europe. This meant choosing to continue climbing the corporate ladder, or stay in Japan and invest in my marriage.

Guess what I chose?

I turned fear into courage and stepped into the unknown. I quit that high-paying corporate job, packed my bags, and made the move to

Japan a permanent one. Choosing my marriage wasn't a tough decision, but with my husband in the U.S. Navy and constantly deployed, what followed was a complete nightmare. I had no job, no friends, no family around, and no neighbors who spoke English. I felt like a total failure, and wondered if I'd made a huge mistake. Memories of the deep dissatisfaction I felt during childhood started to haunt me, but Mom wasn't there to shout at me, to tell me to get back on my feet and stop feeling sorry for myself.

Eventually I got to the lowest point of my life, where I felt there was no other option but to cry. Yes, I'm a warrior, but I'm also human. And while corporate life wasn't perfect, it had been fulfilling for me. I went from launching product lines and creating and implementing marketing strategies for twenty-four countries to managing house-cleaning and meal-planning for one.

At the verge of depression, filled with uncertainty and nursing a hurt ego, I started freelancing. Freelancing filled a big void in my life while I lived in Japan and started to shape my new professional identity. Then, when we moved back to the United States, I started working for an employer who constantly implied I wasn't a good digital marketer, but kept demanding more and more hours from me. I recognize now that the constant criticism was his way of making me feel small while his company's earnings grew from sixty thousand to almost one million dollars per quarter during the year I was the only marketing person there. Even though it was a freelancing gig, I was deeply frustrated with the work environment. On top of that, I worked fifty-plus hours each week, and I had to leave my baby at daycare. It became clear I was leading a life that didn't align with my values. That's when I knew it was time to quit freelancing.

You'd think that realization would have set me free, yet when I decided to start my own company, self-doubt was running high. Striking out on my own was so different from the other key decisions I made, and this time, I felt like I was shooting in the dark. I opened that LLC and couldn't bring myself to advertise my services for months. I was terrified, constantly wondering if my former boss had been right about me all along. What if that company's success wasn't actually a result of my hard work, but a fluke?

Then I learned that those negative voices never leave us alone…ever. I learned that in order to overcome self-sabotage and imposter syndrome, you need to acknowledge these voices and choose a new path forward for yourself.

Some personal development gurus say that what drives people to succeed is either inspiration or desperation. Whether you are inspired or desperate, I believe awareness is the first step toward understanding how your decisions shape your destiny. There will be times when you have no control, but if there is one thing you can be certain of, it's that life happens. Beating yourself up, complaining, or cursing those around you won't help you change your circumstances. The only thing you can really control at any given moment is how you feel, and the weight you give to those feelings.

So, when things get tough, start paying attention to how you react. If you feel lost, stuck, or overwhelmed, check in with your soul about what your options are—because when you believe that you're the *creator* of your reality, rather than a spectator, you will inevitably behave differently. When you're aware of the weight of your choices, you'll find yourself being bolder and more decisive. And when you're confronted with a new challenge, it's important to ask yourself: Who do I have to become to make this happen?

When I decided to start my business, I had to become a CEO. And this time—unlike that moment back in middle school!—I was able to find role models all around me. I looked up to other courageous women in business, and they inspired me. They uplifted me. They gave me hope that anything was possible. Then, instead of giving in to my imposter feelings, I decided I wanted to *be* like one of them. I didn't need anyone's validation or permission to step into my power, and neither do you.

I want you to know that your destiny isn't written in stone. You can look at your reality today and listen as it screams, "Holy crap! You're never going to get out of this!" But you can also turn inward, and listen carefully to the whispers of your heart. This may sound like praying, or asking for God's inspiration, or simply listening to your intuition. Either way, I believe that stepping into your power is nothing more than giving yourself permission to explore the unknown and listen to your heart's whispers. It's about feeling scared or uncertain and still having the courage to do something about it.

There will be moments when you have to take a big leap of faith and do something outside of your comfort zone. But most of the time, we just have to overcome our inner fears, and realize that decisions are not extraordinary events. They can be as small as focusing on the positive, keeping the negative voices of your mind captive, or silencing doubtful thoughts with gratitude. Remember—some days, we will knock on a door, and the answer will be "no." We'll knock on another door, and that will also be a "no." But unless we keep knocking on doors, we'll never hear that "yes!"

My mom taught me that when you're rejected, or when you feel like you're failing, *that* should your motivation to keep going—not a reason to quit. And while I was very frustrated about selling clothes with her then, I now recognize that if she'd never dragged me along with her on those tough days, I wouldn't be the woman I am today. I wouldn't be able to impact my clients' lives the way I do.

So, if you're feeling guilty, scared, desperate, discouraged, or stuck, just keep going. Turn fear into courage and step into the unknown. No matter how many closed doors you've faced or how many times you've felt like you've failed, you haven't! Someday, you'll look back and realize you're on your own journey, and you'll be able to connect the dots. *Decide* to step into your power and truth, own how uniquely amazing you are, and keep going.

About the author: Giselle Grant is an award-winning marketing strategist and business coach. She helps unstoppable girl bosses grow profitable businesses and change the world without sacrificing their values. With an MBA from the University of Virginia, fifteen years of experience working at Forbes 500 companies, and a candid tough-love approach to coaching, she ensures her clients get results.

Giselle is known as a brand-whisperer and life-changer. Her proprietary growth strategy method has helped several business owners cross the six- and even the seven-figure mark.

You can find her latest project at gisellegrant.com or on Facebook at facebook.com/growwithgiselle.

Unapologetic

by Christine Lu Singh

Growing up, I often felt like the odd one out. I was the chubby, nerdy kid with a wild and creative imagination who preferred to stay in during recess rather than play outside like everyone else. My Asian immigrant parents weren't around much as they were working hard to provide for our family, largely leaving me to navigate various milestones and childhood obstacles on my own. As an only child, I spent a lot of time on my own while my parents were working. To keep me busy, they enrolled me in every single enrichment class they could find—Chinese school, piano, singing, art, math, dance. You name it, I was there.

From the age of four up until I turned nine, I was part of a dance troupe that would perform locally in our city. We were a group of ten or so, and I was often thrown into the spotlight as the solo singer. It wasn't something that I enjoyed doing, but I went along with it to please my parents. This meant lots of hard work on my part, with hours of dance and singing practice in the evenings and weekends. As a result, I feel that I lost out on key parts of my childhood—like learning how to ride a bicycle, which is still a regret I have today.

Being part of that dance troupe is also the first memory I have of being bullied by my peers. I didn't understand why they teased me so relentlessly, but it felt like I had a target on my back. Now, I realize this was one of those foundational moments in my childhood where I learned a limiting belief that I would carry into the rest of my life. I made the false association that being the center of attention led to hurt, pain, and abandonment from my peers.

I remember another time in grade school when a good friend of mine was upset. She sat our group of friends down and read us a letter where she shared feelings of being left out. In that letter, she specifically called me out as the cause of this. While I can now applaud the maturity she had to articulate and communicate her feelings so clearly, at the time, I didn't know how to be on the receiving end of it. I took it personally, as some kind of attack on my personality—that I was "too much" or "hogging all the attention." This situation reinforced the painful belief I'd learned earlier in my childhood, and I internalized that belief, making the decision to dim my own light so that others wouldn't feel uncomfortable in my presence.

As a young child, it was hard for me to understand why this was happening. I just wanted to be me—to be accepted for who I was. I wanted to be seen for the creative and unique talents I had. And aside from the occasional rebellion as a teenager, I was always the good girl. I listened to my parents, did my homework, completed school with honors, and was accepted into a respectable university. But when I look back on my years as a school-age kid between four and seventeen, I realize I never truly came out of my shell. Instead, I always fit myself into the boxes that others were so quick to place me in. I didn't understand it then, but I was conforming to those around me to make *them* feel more comfortable, without understanding the inherent cost to myself.

When I attended university, I finally experienced the taste of new beginnings and the freedom that I had been craving. With a whole new campus to explore and thousands of students who didn't know me yet, I felt I was given the gift of restarting my life and redefining who I wanted to be. In a short time, I found myself involved with a number of student-run organizations, and I began to shine again as I was appreciated for who I was.

But once a pattern is learned, it's hard to shake it off. Those unhealed wounds have a way of reappearing in your life until you have a chance to work through them. Time and time again, those self-limiting beliefs of mine would rear their ugly heads, and I would take another step back, further and further away from the spotlight. This was true both at university and in the years that followed. I spent the first decade of my career climbing the corporate ladder in the world of marketing and public relations. I'd often find myself playing it small, internalizing a lot of the stress and pressure I encountered in my day-to-day work. I was still playing the role of the "good girl" who accepted things the way they were, rather than standing up for myself and challenging the norm.

In the last few years of working in my PR role, I finally realized how unhappy I was with my life. While it seemed like I had everything right on paper, with a successful career at a world-renowned agency, I would wake up each morning with a feeling of dread before going into the office. I was no longer finding joy in my work, nor being heard or seen for my creative ideas. It seemed as if I was no longer adding value, and everything in my life felt like an uphill effort.

During this stressful time, I also experienced a flare up with my chronic hives, which was something I'd been battling since I was a teenager. They'd suddenly appear in my life, usually triggered by times of monumental stress, and would last for months. I'd seen every type of doctor you can think of, from allergists to dermatologists to nutritionists, and no one could ever give me a reason why the hives kept showing up or prescribe effective ways to keep them at bay. Driven by frustration, I started looking beyond western medicine for answers. A coworker of mine suggested I consider seeing an energy healer she'd found, who had been helpful and supportive in her own time of need. I had no idea what to expect, but with a curious mind and an open heart, I decided to book a session with her.

What followed was a free-flowing conversation that allowed me to share what was on my mind. Within that first meeting, she was able to tune into my feelings of being lost and swimming upstream. She also pointed out right away that I wasn't working in a job that was right for me—it wasn't aligned with my soul's purpose on earth. At first, I felt a lot of resistance toward this message. It wasn't a concept that I was consciously ready to face. Nevertheless, a seed was planted that day, and while I had no way of knowing this then, the dots would eventually connect in ways that I never could have imagined.

In an effort to find ways to minimize my stress levels on my own, I decided to give meditation a try. I found an incredible studio that offered all types of meditation, such as Chakra Balancing, EFT Tapping, Yoga Nidra, Shamanic Journeys, and Breathwork. I walked into my first Breathwork class thinking we were just going to be focusing on our breath during meditation, but it turned out to be so much more than that. Breathwork is a form of active guided meditation, often paired with a carefully curated playlist designed to open your heart and mind, along with inspirational guidance from the facilitator. It can be a very somatic experience, as it helps you remove any stuck or stagnant energy in the body, leaving you feeling energized or relaxed.

After my first experience with Breathwork, I felt cramping in my hands and feet and an intense sensation in my stomach that I'd never encountered before. It felt like something was *alive* within me, a force that was twisting and pulling. The instructor enthusiastically clasped her hands and said it was likely that my solar plexus was activated. She went on to say my creative spirit was trying to communicate with me and I should *listen* to her.

Our lives are made up of a series of defining moments, and that first class would change the course of my life forever. On that day, another seed was planted, encouraging me to continue following my curiosity and discovering more about my true purpose on earth in this lifetime. I began a journey of self-discovery, diving deep into learning all I could from a spiritual perspective. I stepped out of my own way and allowed the universe to guide me from one lesson to the next.

Breathwork became an integral tool in my self-care practice. I found that within one's spiritual journey of awakening, it was important to have an open mind, to explore without any expectations. I started attending all types of meditation classes, often seeking out Breathwork specifically, and the growth and discovery was magnificent. It allowed me to reconnect with the scared little girl inside me, to let her know that she was safe and give her what she needed so that she felt heard. In this way, I cleaned out years of conditioning, of old stories that had been imprinted on me when I was young as the result of something that someone had once said. I was finally able to break free, to see what was my truth and release what was not.

Within a couple of months, this soul-searching gave me the clarity I needed to realize I was not living a life that was true and authentic to my soul. I decided to take a leap of faith and leave my corporate job, without much of a plan. I was terrified, but I knew in my heart that I was making the right decision.

Stepping out to create a business all on my own brought up all types of feelings. One of the biggest challenges I had to quickly face (and, truthfully, am still learning to overcome) was how to push beyond the limitations I'd set for myself. I read *The Untethered Soul* by Michael A. Singer, which taught me that we create our own boxes from what we think is possible. When we reach the edges of these boxes, we can quickly become paralyzed with fear. In those moments, we have a choice of pushing through, or retreating back into our comfort zone. Luckily, I've found that working through fear is like building a muscle. The more I embraced my self-imposed boundaries and pushed past my fears, the easier it became the next time. This left me with a thrilling and empowering feeling once I overcame what I'd once thought was impossible.

I also had to learn how to let go of the opinions of others. As a recovering people-pleaser, this is something that I'm always working on—reminding myself that I'm not limited by what others' opinions. And, finally, I learned how to trust in the overall journey. Not knowing how things will work out, but still having faith in the process, is the only way to keep going after my dreams, day after day.

After thirty plus years of playing it small, I'm proud to have chosen an unconventional path where I experience freedom and autonomy every day. I now have a very flexible working schedule that's more in tune with the ebb and flow of my energy. I exercise healthy boundaries and no longer work with clients who aren't aligned with my soul's purpose and mission. And, perhaps most importantly, I hold open safe, no-judgment spaces for others to explore their own desires and their shadows.

In the short time since I became an entrepreneur, I've learned many lessons, allowing joy to guide me on my path. I've been paying attention to what makes my heart happy and fills me up with energy, and what activities or interactions leave me feeling drained. I've been focused on breaking away from the "shoulds" of life, and following my joy as my compass instead. Now, it's my intention to pass what I've learned along to you, with journal prompts for reflection, in the hope that you will experience the freedom you are worthy of.

***

Reflect on these questions: **What activities truly excite you? What activities leave you feeling drained?**

Our bodies hold a lot of wisdom and can inform us how we feel about a situation without recognizing it consciously. After a long day, I review what's taken place and take note of how my body feels as I reflect on a particular moment or interaction. Am I feeling tension? Or is there lightness and expansion? Tuning into these physical cues can be a powerful message from our bodies.

Reflect on these questions: **How are you micromanaging your life? Are there places where you can release your grip?**

I have taken a major step back from being a Type A planner who leaves nothing to chance. I now understand the importance of having space to breathe, and have witnessed so many miracles happen when I'm in flow. It takes a lot of practice, time of self reflection, meditation, and there is always more to do.

Reflect on these questions: **What are you grateful for in your life at the moment? For a daily practice, start and end your day by stating out loud or writing down three things you are grateful for.**

Practicing gratitude is one of the most simple and effective tools to call more abundance and magic into your life. When you don't know what you want to manifest, sharing appreciation for what you do have in your life will allow more of the positive energy to flow toward you.

Reflect on these questions: **When was the last time you slowed down and gave yourself some "me" time?**

Giving myself time and space to reflect has allowed me to create a lot of space in my life. This can look however it feels comfortable for you: journaling, meditation, or even just taking a bath with no distractions. I've learned how to tune into my inner voice and let my intuition speak (which isn't easy to do, as it can be as quiet as a whisper). Trust and follow the wisdom within you. It's always there guiding you; we just aren't trained to listen to it.

Reflect on these questions: **What could you do for hours and it feels like no time has passed? What have you been complimented on in the past?**

I encourage you to take an assessment of your own unique gifts by asking five to ten people in your personal network to share what they feel are your natural talents. Often we can't see what our most obvious talents are because they come so easily to us that they're second nature, and we think it's something that everyone else is good at, too.

***

I am so humbled and honored by the community of soul-seekers that I've connected with over the last few years, who are opening up to this world of self-discovery and alternative healing. Whether we are consciously aware of it or not, we all carry baggage from the conditioning we were exposed to during childhood. Experimenting with different healing modalities has allowed me to shed and break out of the boxes that I was confined to for so long. Now, I see life as a beautiful quilt, with each square representing a different piece of the story that we're sewing together, one at a time. We may not know what the bigger picture will look like at the end, so it's important to have trust and faith that all our experiences are essential building blocks as we move through life. None of the opportunities I've had would've come my way if I didn't follow my own intuition about what sparked my joy, and life has proven to me time and time again that if you want something bad enough, you can truly make it happen.

This is just the beginning of my journey, and there's still so much more to come. Wherever you might be on yours, I hope you have found some solace and inspiration, and that the following words might help you move from a place of fear to a place of love. Try speaking them out loud, and allow the message to resonate deeply into your being—and feel free to substitute any of these words with those that are more applicable to your situation.

I am tired. I am tired of playing it small. I am tired of being put into boxes that don't fit. I am tired of making myself smaller to make others feel comfortable. I am tired of people telling me what I can or can't do. What I am or am not capable of. I am tired of dimming my light.

I am ready. Ready to take up space. To move away from my comfort zone. To let the light in.

I am ready to be UNAPOLOGETIC. Unapologetically **me***. I have lived enough years in the shadow of fear, of being terrified to disappoint others.*

What if I was told that it is MY JOB to first not disappoint MYSELF, even if it means disappointing others in the process?

What if I was told that I COULD NOT FAIL? That all I need to do is focus on taking that first step, and the next step after that?

What if I was told that others' definitions of me do NOT define me?

It's safe for me to embody all of who I truly am.

It's safe for me to take up space and own my uniqueness without apology.

It's safe for me to shine my light as bright as it wants to be, touching all corners of this earth.

It's safe to be UNAPOLOGETICALLY ME.

I am WORTHY.

I am LIGHT.

I am FREE.

About the author: After a decade of building a successful career in public relations and marketing, Christine Lu Singh decided to take a leap of faith and left the corporate world behind to pursue what lit her soul up the most.

With her love of bringing people together, she began to curate unique experiences, inspiring people to awaken their intuition by tapping into their inner joy through intuitive arts and crafts, mindful cooking, meditation, tarot readings, sister circles, and more.

Christine is passionate about supporting people on their healing journeys and offers Breathwork sessions, intuitive readings, and distance reiki energy healing. Join Christine on a self-healing journey to remember your natural gifts and rediscover the magic you already have within.

You can view her latest project at www.breathewithtine.com or on Instagram at @breathewithtine.

Triumph

by Michele Duhigg

It was the summer of 2015 and I had just put my two young daughters to bed. My husband was working the night shift, so I'd planned to spend the next couple hours catching up on email and browsing the internet before heading to bed myself. I pulled up our browser history to try and find a website I wanted to revisit when I saw something that literally took my breath away.

It was a record of an explicit text message sent from my husband's phone. But it wasn't sent to me—it was sent to a number I didn't recognize.

The investigator in me kicked in full-force, and I spent the next several hours searching for answers. I discovered the number belonged to a woman he worked with, and there had been a lot of flirtatious banter between the two for months now. It seemed somewhat innocent at first, but built up to more direct, sexual messages that suggested the two were physically intimate.

I was in complete shock. We were married at twenty-two years old, and even though our marriage had been rocky on and off for the last ten years, I never thought infidelity would be something we would face. How could he be unfaithful after everything we'd overcome together?

To many, our relationship likely seemed doomed from the start. We were high school sweethearts, but my longing to discover my higher calling led me to being trapped in a cult for more than half of my college years, where I was forbidden to see or talk to him. It was a very emotional, confusing time, and in spite of his best efforts to convince me to choose him—and as much as I wanted to—the church convinced me our relationship was a sin. So I cut him out of my life.

Two years later, I realized I had been brainwashed and was ready to escape the religious prison that had held me hostage. Naturally, I ran straight back to him—the only person I thought might understand what had happened to me. At first, I wasn't sure how to reach out, but when I finally decided to send a simple *Happy New Year!* text, he immediately responded with enthusiastic curiosity about why I was contacting him after all this time. A couple days later, we met for a three-hour lunch, and six weeks after that, we were engaged. I was thrilled, but a lot had happened during the two years we were apart, and even though we seemed to pick up right where we left off, we were both very different people and had each experienced emotional trauma.

Still, we did our best to mask those lost years and start over. We did all the things a couple should do: We got married. Bought a house. Took vacations. Had kids. Worked hard. And we were happy enough, I guess. But the stresses of life were definitely weighing on us. We struggled financially. We typically worked opposite schedules and, as any parent knows, having two young kids meant we were always stressed out and tired. So, no, we didn't put much effort into our relationship, but I never thought he would look elsewhere for comfort and affection. Somehow I believed we could continue on the way we were, get the kids off to college, and *then* work on our marriage. Of course, that meant I had accepted the idea of being in a lackluster marriage for the next fourteen years, but I had never even contemplated divorce.

The perfectionist in me was defeated. I prided myself on being all the things—wife, mother, career woman, chef, housekeeper, chauffeur—but in that moment, I felt empty. Worthless. Like I had never been good enough. I lost sight of the passionate, purposeful, inspired, spiritual woman I once was.

I went through all five stages of grief over the next few months: denial, anger, bargaining, depression, and acceptance. That night and for the next few days, I was in complete denial, but that denial quickly turned to rage. At him. At the other woman. At myself, for being so foolish. I had spent the last ten years taking care of him, building a home for our children, and denying my inner calling to be the wild and free warrior I knew I was meant to be. And he decided to throw that all away for someone else? Who did she think she was? And how was I so oblivious?

Then I bargained with him: how could we fix our marriage? I gave him more love and attention than I had in years. We went to couples' therapy and spent hours talking about where things went wrong and how we could pave a new way forward. But through it all, I knew that our trust was broken, and things would never be the same. Sure, we could attempt to "fix" our marriage, but the next time he was running late, I would wonder if he was with another woman—and I would likely take advantage of the opportunity to make him feel guilty about it all over again.

I knew I couldn't live like that. I fell into depression and felt like the world was closing in on me. I spent hours at night crying and feeling sorry for myself. I wasn't sure how I was ever going to pull myself out of it. It was about five months later that we agreed our marriage was over. The day he moved out, I literally felt a weight lifted off my shoulders. I was finally free—free from all of the expectations I had allowed to rule my life for so many years. Free from the emotional roller coaster I had been riding. Free from the frustration, pain, and heartache that had filled too many of my days. And I was excited for my future.

I was ready to start over again. I wanted to learn who I was as a woman—not as a wife or a mother, but as an individual. So I dove in head-first, and found myself on a spiritual journey like nothing I had ever experienced before.

This time, it wasn't about looking outward to find the missing piece in my life. It was about looking inward to discover who I was and what I wanted. It was about identifying my own skills, talents, and passions, and then being authentic with those around me. I spent a lot of time hiking, thinking, praying, and meditating, and it wasn't long before I realized that I had been living my life to please others while failing to be true to myself. I knew I could live my life on my own terms rather than simply doing the things that were expected of me—I just had to figure out how.

I became obsessed with personal development and read countless books and articles on the habits of successful people, so I could adopt them as my own. I listened to podcasts, took self-development courses, worked with coaches, and started to build the confidence I needed to step into the power within myself. I gained clarity on my goals and a new commitment to making them happen. I created a vision board to remind myself of what I was working toward, and I spent time imagining what it would feel like to make those things happen in my life.

Once I harnessed the power of clarity, intentionality, and imagination, my life changed fast. Within two years, I bought a new car and a new house, and I met a wonderful man who is now my husband. I was happy, but as it turns out, my divorce wasn't the last of the challenges I would face.

In 2019, to my total shock, I was laid off from my corporate job. I had heard of other people at my company losing their jobs, but I figured I was safe. I'd spent the last eight years acting as the right hand to the practice leader, after all. I was the glue that held the team together. But just like that, I found myself starting over in life—*again*.

This time, though, I knew I didn't want to put my future in another employer's hands. I'd always felt that I was called to do more—to help other women, particularly. And my countless challenges, which had forced me to start over multiple times, had given me the perfect experience to stand on.

So I started a coaching business to empower women to take control of their lives and go after what they wanted—just as I had done in my own life. *Several times.* As women and caretakers, we tend to live small, keeping ourselves busy and burying the idea that there's more to life. We hide behind our self-appointed responsibilities and convince ourselves it would be selfish if we put ourselves first. But why? Because we're afraid of our own greatness? Or is something else holding us back?

I had personally overcome enough obstacles in life to know what it took to use those challenges to become stronger, wiser, more resilient, and more aligned with who I'm meant to be. Because of that, I was able to pull together my Three Keys to Overcoming Obstacles. I've used this framework countless times in my own life, and I want to share it with my fellow soul sisters and warrior goddesses so you can turn your trauma into triumph—like you deserve! The three keys are:

Reflect.

Reset.

Rewire.

The first step is to **Reflect**. Reflection is key to overcoming obstacles. Most of us have deep-rooted, limiting beliefs that were embedded into our subconscious when we were young. You see, as children, our Reticular Activating System (RAS)—our brain's filter—categorizes everything we experience into "hurtful" or "helpful" buckets, even before the brain is fully formed and able to recognize anything deeper than what we see right in front of us. When we fast-forward to adulthood, more often than not, we're still held back by some silly thing that happened when we were seven years old, because we never took the time to ditch that belief and replace it with a new one. That means we, as adults, must intentionally dig up our insecurities and break apart any false "truths" we may be holding onto.

Take me, for example. In my first-grade class, we were allowed to invite our parents to help us decorate gingerbread houses during the Christmas season. I was so excited for my mom or dad to help me crush the competition, but they both told me they had to work and couldn't come to the gingerbread house day at school. I was crushed, and my seven-year-old brain interpreted their choice to work instead of come to school with me to mean I wasn't worthy. As a result, I spent the next twenty-five years searching for acceptance, living my life for others, and never feeling good enough.

Once I took the opportunity to look back at that gingerbread house scenario from a neutral perspective, I realized it wasn't about their lack of love for me or that I was unworthy of their time. My parents both worked full-time jobs and were doing the best they could to provide a great life for my brother and me. What a powerful revelation! I'm so thankful I participated in one of Jack Canfield's meditation sessions to help me reflect and discover the "truth" that had distorted so many years. I was finally able to let go of that limiting belief and start building a healthier relationship with my parents.

What about you? Are there any impressionable moments from your childhood that have fed your present insecurities? Allow yourself to reflect on your past, to understand your story and how it unfolded. Take responsibility for anything you may have done, or interpreted incorrectly, and release whatever is blocking you from true peace and happiness. When you can accept that culpability, and release the emotional trauma attached to the event, you will finally be set free from the things that have been holding you back. When you shift your perception, you will move from living in fear to living in love—and you will find the necessary confidence to step into the power within yourself.

Once you disconnect yourself from your limiting beliefs, and you take back the power you gave up for so long, you have the freedom to decide what you want your future to look like. This is where you **Reset**. What are your goals? What do you want to accomplish? Who do you want to become? Now is the time to decide.

I specifically recall deciding to be the best mom I could be as a result of my failed marriage. Up until that point, I had good days and bad days with the girls. When I was in the moment with them, my heart was full of love and joy, but then I would get sucked back into all the unrealistic expectations of what a good mother "should" be. The resulting stress would leave me tired, frustrated, and short-tempered with my daughters, which in turn fed an endless cycle of guilt for not being "enough."

The day I decided to be intentional with my daughters completely changed my relationship with them. It has been more than five years since then, and I am proud to have cultivated a close-knit, honest, and trusting bond with them that can never be broken. My girls know they can be themselves with me, and even though we may need to have tough conversations sometimes, they know I will always love them and have their best interests at heart. I'm so grateful that was one of the many decisions I made as I was resetting my life and the course I wanted it to take. Because I committed myself to that decision, I was able to match up my external reality with what I wanted inside.

You can do this, too! Use your reclaimed power to decide what you want in life. Be intentional about your goals and commit to making them happen. Recognize that your problems won't disappear immediately, but staying connected to your "why" and aligning your life with your authentic self will keep you on the right path and moving forward.

Finally, it's time to **Rewire**. In order to stay the course, you need to elevate your thinking. Shift your negative thought patterns to positive ones. Intentionally choose what you want to think, feel, and believe rather than defaulting to what comes naturally or what you've done in the past. For example, have you ever driven home from work, and when you finally arrived, you couldn't remember how you got there? That's because your brain loves to work on autopilot. This is due to something called implicit memory, which is ingrained, automatic, and habituated. This is also how our limiting beliefs become so deeply lodged after years of reinforcement.

Here's the science behind it: Neurons that fire together, wire together. Your habituated thoughts (beliefs) are wired responses in your brain. They work through associations, meaning a particular person, location, topic, or thing that is tied to a certain memory and/or emotional state. This association, at a physical level, is a neuron connection or "wire" in your brain that connects the "thing" to the emotional memory. When we're exposed to that stimulus—whether thinking about it or experiencing it—the brain automatically follows the wire from that "thing" to the thoughts and emotions associated with it. Your brain likes to be efficient, and it's specifically designed to make these connections so that you can quickly interpret and respond to future life experiences.

Over time, the neural network in your brain is literally rewired through repetition—which means that *we* can choose what we want to believe! So let's fill our brains with positive, empowering thoughts rather than negative, victimizing ones.

Are you in? Here's how we do that.

Elevating our thinking can be accomplished with several different tools and techniques. Gratitude is key in helping us become more positive and thankful for the little things. Affirmations enable us to replace old, limiting beliefs with new, empowering ones. Visualization helps us clarify exactly what we're working toward. Mindfulness—achieved through meditation, journaling, yoga, and other practices—is crucial for staying centered and aligned with our source energy.

Once you're more aware and intentional about the thoughts, feelings, and beliefs you're having, it's time to kick it up a notch by tapping into your emotions. Emotion is the accelerator to manifesting anything. Affirmations and visualization are the first piece of the puzzle, but using your imagination to evoke excitement is the next powerful step.

I remember sitting in my office in the new home I bought for myself and my girls after my divorce. I was staring at my vision board and feeling butterflies in my stomach over all the exciting things I was planning for our lives. It was so powerful, and as I made more time to do that, the more that excitement stuck. It was only a matter of months before many of the things on my vision board came true, and through several variations of my vision boards since, I've been able to manifest many positive changes in my life. The list has included physical things (new cars, houses, RVs, money), experiences (vacations, adventures), life goals (becoming a published author), accolades (recognition, awards), and more.

It hasn't all fallen into my lap, though. I had to work toward my goals every day. But through clear, decisive, inspired action, I now wake up with a passion and purpose for life each morning. I am so grateful for all my blessings, but I also realize it's through intentional inner work that I've gotten to where I am. I dug through a lot of insecurities to create the confident belief that I am worthy of achieving my dreams, and I have tapped into my spiritual energy to remain inspired and motivated to keep going day after day.

It hasn't been easy—fear and doubt still creep back in every now and then. But now, I am equipped with the necessary tools to replace those thoughts with ones that align with my new beliefs. And knowing I am surrounded by my loving husband, family, and friends, and living a life of freedom and fulfillment, is a dream come true!

And if I can do it, so can you. Here are some tips you can try: Make a "joy" list. Write down the simple things that bring you joy, and make time for at least one of those things every day.

Create a list of affirmations that speak to the areas of your life you struggle with the most and commit to saying them every day for thirty days. Since the brain loves confidence bias, it will look for ways to support your new affirmations, and you'll start to form new beliefs in no time!

Get visual. Search the web for guided visualizations or for specific help with making your own vision board. Spend time looking at your goals each day and imagine what it would feel like to make those dreams a reality.

You may find yourself in a place of starting over, like I have many times. Just take each day one at a time, and do something each day that moves you closer to your goals. Believe you deserve it, and it will be yours.

Everything you need is right inside you. All you need to do is invest in yourself, so you can stop doubting, boost your confidence, and create an authentic life that fills you with joy!

About the author: Michele Duhigg is a certified life coach who specializes in mindset, law of attraction, and manifestation techniques to help women overcome obstacles and create a purpose-led life of fulfillment, freedom, and abundance!

Despite encountering numerous challenges in life, Michele's Three Keys to Overcoming Obstacles has enabled her to not only overcome, but use those experiences to become stronger, wiser, and more aligned with who she is meant to be.

Michele was named a 2020 Woman of Influence by Amazing Women Media and has been featured in *Thriving Women* magazine, the *Amazing Women of Influence 2020* book, *Voyage Phoenix* magazine, and AZ Big Media. She co-authored the book *You Can Have It All* and is a contributing author to Thrive Global and Elephant Journal.

You can view her latest project at www.duhiggcoaching.com or join her community at www.facebook.com/groups/wildandfreewarriorsisterhood.

Section 3

Showing Up in Your Life to Unlock the Impact You Can Create

"Your journey begins with a choice to get up, step out, and live fully."

—Oprah Winfrey

33

    This is a long-held belief of mine: There's no such thing as failure. There is only the lesson to be learned from not achieving your desired outcome.

    We are going to grow disheartened. We are going to lose sight of our goals. We are going to get down in the dumps, ugly crying on the floor because things aren't going the way we planned them.

    There will be days when you will feel like crap and unworthy. But let those days inspire you to keep moving forward.

    Let those days swell you up with infectious energy.

    Let those days empower you to shatter that glass ceiling.

    Let those days force you to rise above the status quo.

    I know you have a deep passion rooted directly in your soul.

    YOU will make a difference. YOU will make an impact.

    And if you ever have any doubts: The Rising Sisterhood is here for ***you.***

Abundance

by Charmaine Johnson-Fuller

In 2012, I was a stay-at-home mom of three: two school-aged children with special needs, plus an infant. I was also trying to tape together a marriage that was falling apart. We didn't hate each other yet, but we didn't like each other very much, either. And as if all that wasn't enough, I'd recently started a handcrafted card business. I loved making cards and the joy they brought to people's lives, but the amount of pressure I put on myself to be a successful entrepreneur, parent, and wife began to eat away at me—and the stress I felt on a daily basis caused my life to unravel.

I honestly don't know how I survived these years, because I was running on fumes, wine, coffee, and lots of sugar. Each day, I would stumble into the bathroom for a brief moment and wonder, *How in the world did I get here?* Those moments didn't last long, though, because I couldn't even go to the bathroom in peace. There was always a kid in there with me, talking or crying, and I seriously thought I was going to lose my shit on a daily basis.

My day always started with taking care of everyone else in the house. I would get my two oldest children off to school as quickly and efficiently as possible, with the hope of having six hours of freedom to slay the endless to-do list I'd created for myself that day. The problem was that my to-do list was packed tighter than a can of sardines, and I would only ever get to number two or three on my list before a bill collector called, or I remembered an unfinished task from the day before. My ability to stay focused was non-existent, because "shiny object" distractions came in so many different forms.

After each diversion, I would attempt to get back on track, but then another need would pull me away. Before I knew it, it would be time to pick my older kids up from school. It felt like no matter how I planned my day, it would somehow veer off track, and I would end up with more stuff on my to-do list than I started out with. My six hours of "freedom" flew by faster than I could blink, because I didn't realize how much time I spent in the drop-off/pick-up line at school, or the hours my random bursts of volunteering were costing me. I wasn't clear about what my life needed, so I ended each day feeling depleted of my time and energy.

Once I was back home and all three kids were settled, I would start dinner and attempt to make the house look semi-presentable before my husband got home from work. Back then I made elaborate *Food Network*-style dinners that had lots of prep and lots of clean-up, all of which I did alone. I wanted it to seem like I was productive and not just watching soaps and eating snacks all day, but to be honest, I zoned out a lot because I was so overwhelmed with my schedule.

After dinner, I started getting the kids ready for their showers and for bed. Thankfully, this routine was going well for me. I had the kids on a strict bedtime schedule, and much to my relief, they were usually good about following it. Once they were in bed, I was up until 1:00 a.m. working on my card business, trying to complete any leftover tasks from that day, and honestly enjoying the peace of being alone. I felt like it was the only time I got to do something I enjoyed—the only time I didn't have to help a child, make a meal, or be a mom.

When I finally made it to bed myself, it would take me an hour to fall asleep, but due to some ongoing health issues, I would wake up with seizures most nights—which meant I was only getting about four hours of sleep. I was a walking zombie, always in pain and on edge, and I had to work increasingly harder just to exist. I was plagued by debilitating headaches that often prevented me from participating in the smallest things. It felt like my brain was in a heavy fog that I couldn't break free of—it was even hard to speak at times, because I couldn't remember words that at one time had flowed easily. This was particularly frustrating, since I'd always prided myself on my intelligence. I was constantly mad at my body for failing me.

I knew how to portray the perfect image, though. On the surface, it looked like I had the perfect life—like I had everything together. My kids seemed well-adjusted and happy, and my husband and I spoke kindly to each other. I ran the special needs parenting group in our school district, was always available to assist with the PTO, and I lived in one of Michigan's most prized zip codes. Outwardly, I was living the dream. Any woman would have loved to have the life I had, but it was literally draining the life out of me.

For three more years, I continued going to bed late, waking up early, and drinking lots of caffeine. My health took a turn for the worse, and sleep became a rare commodity between my seizures and those of my oldest son. I know now that mine were caused by all the constant stress and pressure I was putting on myself to perform at these insanely high levels. I rarely felt like anything was enough—I didn't feel like *I* was enough. In fact, my running joke to myself was, "I can sleep well when I get rich." But I was operating in a constant state of lacking—lack of money, lack of sleep, lack of connection, lack of business, and lack of health.

Finally, I hit rock-bottom with my health. It was a normal night like any other. I went to bed exhausted, my head spinning with thoughts of all I didn't accomplish that day. I woke up a short time later, feeling like I was about to have another night seizure, so I decided to go to the bathroom.

When I woke up, I was face-down on the floor, covered with a blanket, my head on a towel.

As I lay there—body aching, head throbbing, and tongue badly chewed—I surmised that I must have had the seizure I was trying to avoid the night before, but I didn't remember a thing. At that moment, I knew my life had to change. I didn't know how, but I knew there had to be a better way to live.

The next morning, I went online and searched for any book, podcast, or blog that could tell me how to make the craziness in my life stop. I went on a mission to end the stress, the seizures, the loneliness, the exhaustion—all of the things causing me pain. I traded in my romance novels for self-help and mindfulness books. I started digging deep into my childhood traumas and getting clear on why I felt like I always needed to work so hard. Eventually, I realized that I had been telling myself lies for so long that they had become a part of my being.

Everyone works hard.

The only way to be successful is to work hard.

I didn't rest, and I didn't take breaks. I thought that pushing through would help me complete my to-do list, but that was actually what was keeping me stuck. I had bought into the "no rest for the weary" mindset for so long that I believed it was true. As a result, I had built a life that had no breath, no boundaries—no *life* at all!

How was I supposed to find abundance in this life I'd created? Nothing about my existence felt abundant at all. It always felt forced, rushed, and heavy. My entire life was built on me being a self-sustaining island and never part of a team, because there had never been anyone in my life that I could trust or depend on. I had to learn how to begin breaking down that belief system (B.S.) and replacing it with thoughts and actions that supported the life I wanted to create.

Let me tell ya, this journey hasn't been easy. I've had to uncover and explore some truths that my shame, hurt, and anger would have preferred to keep hidden, but hiding those things was eating away at my soul—and no amount of coffee, wine, or overworking could repair that.

I hired a therapist (I've been through a few of them), a spiritual life coach, and a naturopath. I wanted to heal my issues from the inside out and build a better foundation to live on. My therapist told me to purchase a journal, so I could write down thoughts and memories that we could later process using the Emotional Freedom Technique (EFT). She helped me to release the negative charge, so I could replace it with something new. I left each of our sessions armed with an action step, and boy, oh boy, did I follow. I wanted that pain to be gone.

I worked with my spiritual life coach to help me learn how to trust and tap into my highest self. She helped me to see that the universe was working in my favor, and that I was the one who'd created this mess I was living in. At first, I was angry at her, and there were a lot of tears, but I did what she said. By working with her, I was able to begin to discover the real me—not the girl who drank wine because it was offered, like all the other moms who were drinking, but the woman who was okay with saying no.

Over time, working with these two women taught me how to set boundaries and use my voice again—the voice that had been unheard as a child, resulting in the trauma I'd carried over into my adult life. Thanks to them—and a lot of hard work on my part—my life changed drastically over the course of three years. I dropped thirty pounds, stopped having night seizures, and my migraines disappeared. I also quit drinking, as I'd discovered that I never liked it anyway—it was just something I'd done to be accepted. In fact, I'd done a lot of things I wasn't proud of on my quest for acceptance by others. I was always so afraid to show up as myself, because I never felt like I was enough as I was.

But during those three years of self-discovery, I stopped viewing other people as a way to change myself, or to make myself feel worthy. I stopped showing up in a way that I thought would make them feel comfortable, and instead started showing up as my quirky self. And once I embraced who I really was…I began to feel so free and empowered. I'd never known that life could be so rich and full of joy.

Now, I don't want you to get it twisted—it was hard, and I still have work to do. But I'm learning to honor progress over perfection. I'm learning that my life will never be a perfect ten, and that it's okay to make mistakes, because I know I have a support team that has my back—and because this journey to "enoughness" has been worth it.

The amount of freedom that I feel in my life today was something I never thought I would experience while I still had kids in the house.

Whatever your current situation is, you can turn it around. You are enough and worthy of what you desire. I know it feels impossible when all you can see are the obstacles and the mistakes you've made, but let me tell you—it's possible. The flow you want, the money, the joy, the love, the connection…it's all possible. And if you get nothing else from my story, please take away this one thing:

If this messy girl can turn her life around, so can you.

Abundance is all around us, but we're usually so focused on the "lack" in our lives that we can't see it. We've all been in that space—focused on the bad, trying to create the good. But here's what I know for sure: that kind of mindset leads to burnout and a huge chip in your confidence. If you go after what you desire in that way, you will always lose. It will always feel like you're working harder than you should be, and yet you'll still miss the mark.

At this point, you might be asking, "How do I take the situation I'm in and change it?"

I get it—life feels like a runaway train. It feels like you're living the same day over and over, with no hope of creating the joy you desire. But it doesn't have to be that way, and I'm here to show you why.

I took all my knowledge from the books, websites, and courses and created a six-part framework to improve my life and get back on track when life got crazy. This framework helped me stand firm in my "enoughness" and create more time, energy, and focus in my life. I now use this same framework to help other working mommas get their lives in order and drop the overwhelm and stress they're feeling.

The first thing I had to do was create clarity in my life. I had to understand how my life was currently unfolding so I could make goals and plans from a space of power. Until that point, I had been creating my daily to-do lists based on whatever fire was burning hottest in my life. So, I sat myself down and scored my life areas, to get a true assessment of how they were performing versus where I wanted them to be. Creating clarity in my life empowered me to begin making decisions that supported me.

Then I visualized how I wanted my life to feel. For so long, I hadn't trusted how I felt—the only feelings I was in touch with were exhaustion and infinite stress. Doing this was hard, because it forced me to sit down and think about how *I* really wanted to feel. For so long, I'd been fully invested in the feelings and needs of others, and I had put myself on the back burner. The idea of putting myself first felt strange and almost a little selfish, but it has made all the difference in my life.

I took each of my life areas and wrote out three to five ways I wanted to feel in each of them. Then I narrowed down my list to three words that described how I wanted my life to feel. Today, I still use these words as my GPS to remind me to focus on feeling. This doesn't mean that I sit and eat ice cream and binge Netflix all day, but knowing how I want to feel allows me to say "yes" to things that are going to fulfill me as well as get stuff done.

Once I gained clarity about where my life was and how I wanted it to feel, I wrote out a growth goal for each life area. I focused first on those areas that I felt scored low, because I'd learned that if one life area is struggling, it doesn't matter how hard you work in other areas—that one area will drag your entire life down until it's strengthened. I had to remind myself that I was looking to create progress over perfection, and that going for perfect was what got me into the overwhelming mess my life was in. Having these growth goals laid out allowed me to reach them faster, and in a way, that felt good. Although I faced many hard things, I was able to confront them with ease, because I was clear about where I was, where I was going, and how I wanted this process to feel.

Next, I had to clean up the distractions that had infiltrated my life. Confession: I'm a recovering social media addict. For years, I had allowed endless scrolling on Pinterest, Facebook, and Instagram to take over my day. To help overcome this, I decided to keep track of my social media interactions for a week, taking note of how I felt before and after. Doing this allowed me to see my patterns and fix the cause, rather than just adding tracking apps to shut my social media down. I knew that until I got to the root of things, then no matter what tracking app I used, I would inevitably decide to unblock my social media accounts and scroll away. After cleaning up my social media usage, I found more time in my day to take the actions that were getting me closer to my goals. But in the process, I discovered that I still felt like I was falling short in how much time I had.

Then I learned about the concept of time bending, and that packing my day in super-tight the way I had been was merely adding to my stress. It wasn't making me more productive or adding extra time to my day at all. In fact, overscheduling my day was draining my time, because I rarely had space for life's emergencies or for myself, and since I was so tired from working nonstop that I would just take the time anyway. This would throw my schedule off, and I'd be up all night trying to finish my to-do list. It was a vicious cycle—until I discovered the simple method of allocating dedicated space in my day for the unexpected things that life always seems to throw at us. Setting aside that time each day also forced me to only add tasks to my schedule that were moving my life forward in some way or meeting a specific need for my family. This, combined with the elimination of mindless social media scrolling, helped me to stay focused on what was truly important.

Lastly, I used all of these tools to create a daily plan that supported my *life*—not just the stuff I felt like I *had* to do. I was able to create a map for my day that allowed me to see my victories, relish in gratitude, and breathe deeply. Over time, I found myself getting epic shit done consistently while also taking the time to enjoy the life I had created.

Here's a full disclaimer: this is not some magical bean or one-and-done method. This will take constant work, but remember—*progress over perfection*. Taking these steps isn't about getting everything perfect; it's about creating small wins in your life that will allow you to feel empowered. You don't have to do all the steps at once, and you don't have to do them in order. Simply start where you are and with what feels right for you in this instant. Also, get support. Whether from a coach, mentor, therapist, or pastor—build a team that supports you. Use your voice in your family for more than just voicing your pain. It's possible to laugh more, spend more quality time with your family, and still be a boss in your career or in your business.

Find your balance, and know this: *you* are enough.

You don't need to be or do anything extra to be worthy of more time, energy, and joy in your life. Everything you are is enough, and the abundance you seek is already here, waiting for you to slow down and see it.

About the author: Charmaine Johnson-Fuller is a life strategist with The Charmed Life. She works with entrepreneurial moms of children with special needs and shows them how to create more time, energy, and focus in their lives.

Charmaine has partnered with The Family Center of Grosse Pointe/Harper Woods, CARE of Southeastern Michigan, and other platforms that cater to special needs parents and entrepreneurial moms. Charmaine is also a certified life coach with additional certifications in goal-setting and life transformation.

When Charmaine isn't helping other entrepreneurial mammas slay their life goals, she is hanging with her family, playing with her plants, and catching up on her favorite shows.

You can find her latest project at thecharmedlife.me or on Facebook @Charmedwithchar.

Dream Again
By Cassie Kitzmiller

Do you remember playing the childhood game M.A.S.H. with your friends growing up? It's essentially a "fortune-telling" game, played with a folded piece of paper and designed to predict your entire future. If so, you probably recall that the game would not only supposedly determine where you were going to live, but depending on the number you chose, it could also go on to tell you who you were going to marry, how many children you were going to have, and whether or not you were going to live happily ever after. Pretty impressive from a folded piece of paper and a thirty-second rhyme!

While not terribly realistic, this game pretty much summarized how I planned out my life as a young girl. My friends and I all got pretty good at figuring out the system so that we were guaranteed a mansion and marriage to our current crush, with two angelic children and a picture-perfect happily ever after. If anything happened to throw off our calculations, we would obsessively play the game over and over until our perfect future was nailed to the proverbial wall.

It was with this dream in place that I set out "creating" my plan for the future. At the extremely mature age of nine, I was pretty confident I would marry the love of my life upon graduating college, own our first home by age twenty-one, have three children by the age of thirty, and build a successful career as a veterinarian or small business owner.

Fast forward twenty-one years or so, and my life had gone (for the most part) according to plan. I met my future husband during my senior year in high school, and we dated throughout college. A month after graduation, we tied the knot at my dream outdoor wedding in front of a lake with family and friends (and a few too many geese) by our sides. We purchased a house that same year, and I happily settled into nesting and decorating. Our first son came a year later, while I was opening the second location for the home décor business I ran with my business partner and mentor. A few years later, baby boy #2 joined the family, followed soon after by baby boy #3.

Life was good. Correction—life was *great*. I had successfully checked off all the boxes on the "Dream Life M.A.S.H." game I had created in second grade. Now, don't get me wrong—we faced our fair share of trials and challenges along the way. But for the most part, things were falling right into place, and the only thing left to do was sit back and ride off into our "Happily Ever After" with the sunset glimmering in our rearview mirror.

It's at this point that those of you with more life experience than I will tip your heads back and laugh out loud…because you know *exactly* what's coming next.

While growing up as a young girl—and planning out my entire life based on a pretend game with a bunch of other starry-eyed girls—I never once made any plans beyond the age of thirty. I mean, come on, by thirty I would obviously be mature and grown and have everything figured out, right?! I naively assumed that once one reached such a wise age, the hard part of life would be over, any "real" problems would be solved, and all that would be left would be enjoying the ride. Ha!

In reality, hitting the big 3-0 didn't bother me much at all—as far as aging goes, anyway. But realizing I had accomplished all of my childhood goals and had nothing else to strive for...that was discouraging, to say the least. I spent the entire year after my thirtieth birthday planning up new dream goals to tackle for the next thirty years. Of course, by the end of that time, I would be sixty and finally grown-up enough to know what I was doing—right?!

It was with this success record and confidence at my "amazing ability" to create what I designed for my life that I set out to make my list of goals for the next thirty years. This list included nice, safe goals such as growing my design business, moving into a bigger home for our growing family, and paying off the last of our debt so we could embrace a debt-free lifestyle. I went on a little further from there, but you get the idea—I had new goals for myself, my business, and our family, and I was set!

And then God laughed.

It was only a few months after I completed my "Next Thirty Years" list that I started to realize maybe, just maybe, the Lord had another idea about how these next thirty years were going to go.

Most of my new goals were focused around my career, as I was motivated and ready to take on the world one redecorated living room at a time. I'd originally found my passion for creating beautiful spaces as a fresh-faced seventeen-year-old, when I walked through the doors of a lovely little décor store in historic Jonesborough, Tennessee. I immediately fell in love with the charm and magic of the store and diligently worked my way up from stock girl, to the sales floor, to designer, to partner.

From that original location on Main Street in downtown Jonesborough, my business partner and I opened a sister Christmas shop and then a second location in a neighboring town. As a small shop that carried gifts, home décor, and accessories before the major boom of the online shopping era, we were averaging double-digit growth every year and had no plans to slow down.

The shop and my business partner became a huge part of my personal life as well. They celebrated with me as I graduated college, married my husband, and went on to have our first son. I brought my son with me to work for the entire first year of his life, and he was fondly nicknamed our "shop baby," as all of the ladies took turns caring for him as I worked. I dedicated over ten years to growing the business, and at that point in my life, I was certain the best was still to come! With visions of continued growth and new locations, I was ready to make my next batch of thirty-year goals a reality.

Unfortunately, our sales numbers started showing otherwise. The online shopping era had finally caught on in our small town in Tennessee, and we were suddenly competing in pricing and selection with online mega-brands such as Wayfair, Pottery Barn, and others. In addition to the competition of online shopping, my business partner suffered a major health scare that forced me into taking over a large portion of the management tasks on top of all the design and store responsibilities.

Managing the stores while balancing our growing family started to feel like a weight I wasn't sure I could hold. In the quiet moments—which were few and far between—I started to hear a near-constant voice in my head. Not an actual voice, mind you, but the little whisper that comes from somewhere deep down inside, that you know you've been ignoring for way too long. The voice would occasionally and always very gently whisper, "It is done, but not finished." It always seemed to pop up right when I was in the middle of stressful decisions for the store, or when we started making plans for new locations.

I found myself stomping the voice down, trying to ignore what was becoming more and more clear. While I'd thought my plans for the future were written in stone, it was possible I'd have to let them go and see what else the Lord had in store for me and my family.

During the dark, quiet hours when I sat rocking our youngest son, I would give myself permission to listen to that little voice and wonder, "What if?"

What if we closed the store?

What if I walked away from everything and started anew with no responsibilities?

Then the sun would rise, and I would run around getting the boys ready for daycare. I would rush to work and start all the plates spinning all over again.

This cycle of running, striving, and pushing down the little voice continued on for a few weeks until we got a call that brought everything to a standstill. The owner of the historic home that housed our store needed to sell, and sell fast. We had the option to sign our names over on the dotted line to purchase, or the house was going to go up for sale on the public market.

The moment of truth had come. It seemed as if the entire future of our twelve years of dreams, sweat, blood, and tears had all come down to that one telephone call.

Do we stay, or do we go?

With a big, life-changing decision to be made, my business partner and I did what all good southern women do in times of crisis: we went to lunch.

During that lunch, we poured out our hopes, disappointments, fears, and doubts over hot broccoli-and-cheese soup. We both admitted that taking on a payment as large as the house required was not in our best interests at our current stages of life, and neither one of us could imagine moving the store to another location and starting all over again. I shared with my partner the message that had been bouncing around in my head over and over again during the still moments, and she laughed. Apparently, the voice in her head had been whispering a very similar thing.

Once we laid it all out on the table, and acknowledged that the season we had enjoyed together was ending, it was like a heavy weight had been lifted and we could dream again. During that same lunch—once we acknowledged the "it is done" part of the message—we were excited and encouraged to dream over the "but not finished" portion. We tossed around ideas for another ten or fifteen minutes, then headed back to the store to set the ball rolling on closing a business that had been a staple in our lives for so many years.

The next few months were a whirlwind of calls, sales, packing, and goodbyes. While we knew the decision we'd made was the right one, the daily reminders of the death of a dream can be hard to stomach. Through it all, we were given favor and grace, and at the end of the final closing sale, we loaded the last of the items on the truck, gave everyone a great big hug, and drove off with smiles on our faces and tears in our eyes.

The amazing thing about the death of one dream is that through the pain, sadness, and darkness of putting it to rest, you open your mind to new and exciting dreams that needed the dark to come to life. It has now been three years since that season of change, and I can happily look back and appreciate the growth that has come from the ashes. My former business partner has come full circle and opened an adorable seasonal shop only a few doors down from our old location, where she gives out hugs, advice, and free Hershey's kisses to everyone who crosses the threshold. My own life has opened up in ways I could never have imagined. From writing an Amazon bestselling book, to starting a thriving business-coaching practice, to homeschooling all three boys, I am happily embracing a life of not knowing what's to come.

Not long ago, when organizing some old papers and journals, I came across a copy of my "Next Thirty Years" goals. After a good, long laugh, I started to crumple it up, but I stopped myself. While the goals I set may never be accomplished in the way I had envisioned, I've since learned that when God laughs, there is usually something much better just up the road! So if you find yourself in a similar situation, where your best-laid plans seem to be failing all around you, and you're hearing the whispers of, "It is finished, but not done," here are some words of advice I can share from experience.

First, trust in a higher power that has good intentions for you and your life. Whether you are a believer in Jesus or not, I encourage you to spend some time reading scripture or other encouraging works that will rewire your mind to believe that all detours in our plans are simply bringing us closer to the good plans that are to come!

Second, take time to grieve after a dream comes to an end. Whether it's a dream for your career, a relationship, or something else, grieving loss is an important part of the healing process. Don't skip this step, but don't get stuck here, either. When we closed the shop, I cried, I mourned, and I asked *Why?* several times in the months that followed. But the pain of a dream lost has a way of highlighting what we really value the most, and this clarity often becomes the catalyst for great things to come.

Finally, get up and dream again! Once the season of grieving has lessened, it's imperative to get up and dream again. This process will look different for all of us. In my case, it looked like taking the jump into writing a book that had been a dream of mine since I was a little girl. For you, it might look like taking a new class, reaching out to make a new friend, or even writing out some new thirty-year goals.

The best way to make a new dream a reality is to simply begin. The first steps don't matter so much as just giving ourselves permission to trust in a good future and start dreaming again!

About the author: Cassie Kitzmiller's bestselling books and successful coaching business, CK Designs and Coaching, help women create beautiful living spaces, build lives with lasting impact, and embrace a more fulfilling life. She's been a small business owner for over fifteen years and is an online business leader, a professional speaker, and a NCIDQ-licensed interior designer. Her *Christmas Tree* book made the Amazon bestsellers' list, and her children's books have brought delight to children around the country.

When she is not designing rooms, coaching clients, or encouraging other women of faith on her Christian Women Business Builders Podcast, Cassie can be found homeschooling her three sons or in the kitchen perfecting her chocolate chip cookie recipe.

You can find her latest project at www.cassiekitzmiller.com and discover more about her community for Christian women business owners at www.christianwomenbusinessbuilders.com.

Freedom

By Lucy Liu

The little boy was right beside me when he fell into the hole in the shallow waters. A hole that was so deep, he toppled right in and never came out. At the time, I had no idea what life and death really meant, but I learned on this particular day that water had the power to swallow someone. There was screaming, plenty of crying, and massive panic all around, and what began as a beautiful day at the reservoir quickly turned into a five-year-old's worst nightmare.

I never told anyone this story until I became confident enough to share my fears and open myself up to the world. The memories and details are immensely vague, but the feelings are deeply ingrained. To this day, I experience fear in the face of the clear water of pools, agitation toward the moving currents of the ocean, anxiety over lakes, trepidation for reservoirs, and even dismay at the thought of drinking water. I just felt resentful of any body of water and hated myself for it along the way.

The struggle intensified in high school because a pass on the school's swimming proficiency exam was required for graduation. I practiced for a whole month at my best friend's house for this daunting test, which I was only able to pass by swimming with my head out of the water. Treading water for three minutes and swimming laps with my head raised above the water left my neck strained; it also messed with my back, and my lungs endured substantial pain to the point where I had trouble breathing for the rest of the day.

But my biggest fear besides swimming was the fear of death.

Occasionally in class, I would doodle in my college-ruled notebook—a cement headstone with the big letters R.I.P. on it. Grass crawled around the headstone, and the name was forever forgotten.

I dwelled on the idea of why I feared death for so many years. Could it be because I was scared to experience excruciating pain and suffering? I can't even imagine what patients dying from cancer or other terminal illnesses are feeling, or how frightening it is to face that ending time to come soon. Or could it be that I hate the idea of not having control? Death remains something which we have absolutely no control over. I've always sought control over my life, but I know deep down that birth, aging, sickness, and death are four things in life that can never be controlled by the self. The idea that there is no way to avoid this risk brings chills to my bones.

Thank God I can rule out the fear of eternal punishment. Regardless of my religious or spiritual beliefs, I don't believe I will be punished for what I did in this life. I take every action with the knowledge that I am in full alignment with the results of my actions leading me to a better place in the afterlife.

My conclusion was that my fear was not actually death—it was fear of the unknown, and the notion of being nonexistent. Death is the ultimate unknown in life because no one in the history of human beings has survived it to tell us the reality of what really happens after we take our last breath.

***

Growing up in a traditional Chinese family, I was destined to live the life my parents dreamed for me. They had wonderful jobs in

China, but gave up everything and immigrated to America with high hopes for a better education for me. My mom was once a respected doctor, but because of me, she had to mop floors and clean toilets for others, since she didn't know any English. I *had* to succeed and not let my parents down.

I got straight As and excelled in school.

Music band? I'm in.

Orchestra? Sure thing.

Teacher's assistant? Yes, I'm the best.

Whatever it takes.

When I was in middle school, I took acting lessons and signed with a casting agency. Every single time I went to an audition, the casting director would run out, excited that Lucy Liu was on their list, but their disappointment at seeing me instead was obvious.

"Oh, it's not THE Lucy Liu" is a phrase that continues to ring in my ears decades later, but I love my name, and even decided to keep it after marriage. Still, the limiting belief of my name stuck with me for years. Someone out there was already exceedingly legendary by that name, so surely I would always be nobody. I thought to myself, you certainly don't see another famous Julia Roberts or Angelina Jolie out there, right? It just doesn't happen. And what's worse is I absolutely adore the woman people refer to as "THE Lucy Liu"—she is exceptionally talented as an artist, actress, and director. So, while I can't blame her, I don't want to sabotage myself either.

The struggle is real.

But what exactly is a "limiting belief"? The answer—it is a false belief that we acquire as a result of making an incorrect conclusion about something in life, much like I did about my name. It took me nearly a decade of personal development and self-discovery to overcome that particular belief, as well as other fears of mine. But when I finally embraced the discomfort and stared at my fears head-on, I came out lighter and less fearful. I let go of thinking too much.

Honest clarity lies in letting things go, stepping back, and holding space for the unknown. Being present with contentment and allowing time to pass slowly is part of the healing process. I ceased visualizing the grave and the limitations of my given name, and started visualizing the joyful version of me five years ahead. I shifted my focus to making my life more meaningful and reframed my fears. I told myself repeatedly that *fear* is nothing but "False Evidence Appearing Real."

I practiced acceptance, knowing that fighting any emotion would magnify that exact emotion. Only by practicing acceptance can ease and peace be achieved. Shifting to a mindset of acceptance and abundance allowed me to show up with my attention fully grounded in the present, and experience heightened levels of awareness, happiness, and wisdom.

***

In order to release my limiting belief, I decided to launch my own podcast. But once I made this decision, fear snuggled up to me tightly.

What if people think I'm not qualified to have a podcast?
What if people think I'm riding off the success of her name?
What if people judge me or believe I think I'm better than others?
What if I have zero listeners?

What if I get bad reviews?

The list went on and on forever. Then I remembered what I'd been preaching and blasting all over on the dozen guest podcast interviews I'd joined: I need to reframe this situation. There is always a way, and I have the power to opposite these negatives into positives.

What if people actually relate to my stories?

What if my listeners can't wait to tune in every week to my latest episode?

What if I get messages from listeners about how helpful I was to their lives?

The more I thought about the possibilities, the more determined I was to make these my reality.

Now that I look back on those years, I realize that the constant crush of my self-confidence actually made me *more* confident. I learned an extremely valuable life skill early on—to pick myself up from the floor when I fall. After all, life doesn't get easier; we merely get stronger and more resilient.

Our life journey will always be decked out with pain, risks, laughter, and joy. Honor each season of life, since we can't pick only the seasons of our path that we want to experience. Life is an all-inclusive ride, and learning to acknowledge the fact that there will always be uncertainty will allow our experiences to be more meaningful and joyful, regardless of what life throws at us.

Instead of focusing on the lack of "something," especially the lack of certainty, I started focusing on my abundance. *I am breathing now. I own a house. I own a car. I have clothes and shoes to wear. I am beyond grateful for all that I already have, and I'm going to enjoy today.*

This ex-overachiever and recovering perfectionist let go of the weight of fear and chose to live a thriving life as an unshakable optimist. As a loving wife, motivated mother, and easygoing entrepreneur, I now make it my mission to help women in life transitions go from feeling stuck to full of clarity, with rock-star confidence. Because when we know ourselves, it becomes easier to live a life that's true to our core values. It becomes acceptable to break cultural norms and shatter glass ceilings.

What I wish for you is to do what energizes you for a living and wake up each day with a smile, because another chance for rebirth has been given to you. Feel alive, because the world needs more alive people.

Our circumstances in life are actually neutral—we get to decide if they are positive or negative. We are all natural-born masters of spinning ourselves into negative spirals, but I now pride myself on mastering the skill to pull myself and others out of overwhelm. I am unique and I am somebody, and even if I only help the life of one listener, I will have made my contribution to a better world. I have unshakable faith that I was called to make those contributions, and I will do so for the rest of my life.

And you will, too.

I'd struggled for thirty-three years since that horrific day. Once I broke free, I experienced an immense feeling of liberation and freedom. The positive emotions that flooded my body were astounding, and the mindset change was simply the result of a moment-to-moment shift.

All it takes is one decision. One decision only.

Your life truly changes the exact moment you make a new, aligned, and determined decision. And you—only *you*—have the power to make that decision.

Sometimes it's the smallest decisions that can change our lives forever.

About the author: Lucy Liu is a global business strategist and certified life coach helping high-achieving women in life transitions get unstuck, kiss overwhelm goodbye, cultivate rock-star confidence, see clarity, reach dream goals, and lead joyful, fulfilling lives!

She is an unshakable optimist, wife, mother, easygoing entrepreneur, certified #IamRemarkable women empowerment workshop facilitator, and international motivational speaker.

Lucy also inspires women weekly as the host of her podcast, *The Lucy Liu Show*, which is the fueling station for your mind, business, and life. She has been featured in Medium, VoyageLA, Elephant Journal, ThriveGlobal, and dozens of other media outlets.

You can find her latest project at www.lucyliucoaching.com or on Instagram at @mslucyliu.

Tenacious

by Felicia Ford

I have a reputation for finishing. Even when it involves something I don't want to do, there have been times when completion, finishing, felt like an obligation. This habit has, for the most part, served me well, but when I bite off more than I can chew, it feels like a ball and chain.

Like now, for instance—I just overcame an upper limit problem, which is an occurrence of resistance when you are experiencing growth. It's a moment when your old self and new self collide, sometimes in unexpected ways.

For me, it manifested this time as a minor car accident. My car is relatively unharmed, and I am physically fine. But emotionally? Not so much. Someone backed into me, and it was just enough impact to propel me into some decision-making. Johann Wolfgang von Goethe once said, "By seeking and blundering, we learn." It is the parts of my life that represents my encounters with upper limits.

There are a few things you should know about me: I am an introvert who loves to learn and help people. I sometimes speak in song lyrics, quotes, or stories. I am currently a nonprofit executive director preparing to begin a data fellowship with Harvard University. I am in my fifth month of solo "lockdown," which deserves a soap opera, and I am on the heels of doing a five-day social media challenge on monetization. I call this a "Shift, Pivot, or Stay," as in shift slightly, pivot completely, or do nothing. All of this may sound like more than enough, but it's the right mixture of challenge, creativity, and learning opportunity for me.

I need that right now. My stage exists in a way where I am often balancing subtlety with rigor. It is the intersection of seeking and blundering and learning. I don't always know how and why things happen as they do, but I always trust that things are working for my good—and whether I want it or not, there will be a valuable lesson.

You might be surprised at how many people you look up to who have no idea why they are here. They know they have a skill set to exchange time for currency, and they follow the world's blueprint as the ideal for life and work. There are also people who, more quickly than others, recognize the call to something. They feel an internal pulling for more. You see them, and they often have this uncompromising, insistent resolve. The call may manifest as a side business, a new idea to launch in their work, a new process, a new way of doing, being, or improving. As they attempt to bring this thing to life, they face adversity, yet you still witness their determined drive. These people turn their obstacles into opportunities. They face limitations, restrictions; they slam into the box that attempts to keep them bound. They experience frustration, overwhelm, and incredible experience, and yet, they go on.

I am a part of that group of people, and if you are reading this, I feel that you are, too. Ascribing to this philosophy of life boils down to choice: What if you decide to reject the frustration of being misunderstood, the overwhelm of mundane activities? What if you instead become laser-focused on unleashing the part of you that is driven to create? What happens if you decide to go all the way, no matter the upper limit? What if your intrinsic nature is unshakable, determined, and unrelenting in pursuit? What if you are *inherently tenacious*?

* * *

I love the mountains. I grew up near Charlottesville, Virginia, but it took arriving in Milan in the middle of winter and seeing the Alps to appreciate the views I had back home. Mountains speak to me in a way that inspires peace. Curiosity does that, too. I describe many of my life experiences "as scaling a mountain." Whenever I reached a goal or had some joyful and unexpected encounter, it was a mountaintop experience. If it was a lesson learned in a not-so-great way, it was a valley experience. Regardless, I always have a camera in my hand, a book in my bag, a story to tell, and eyes full of wonder. My desk, my phone, and any keyboard are my entryway to a stage.

But in the middle of my career, this whole mountaintop/valley experience concept didn't exist. I was miserable, and so I changed industries. Shortly after that, I ended a toxic relationship. I ascribed to the world's rules: I showed up early, I did more work. I suffered more than I experienced joy until I shifted to spaces where my creativity could flow—where, when allowed, I could march to the beat of my drum. I began to ask myself, what am I *supposed* to be doing with my life? I was busy helping others with their dreams, their events, and their projects. But I was so. Busy. Doing. And fixing. And helping.

There came a time when *I* desperately needed help. I was sick of it all, but the moment I slowed down enough to ask myself *why*, the more clearly I began to see…the worse things became.

Gaining clarity was not sudden. I naively believed giving my all at work would naturally progress to a reward. I worked seventy, sometimes eighty hours per week, but struggled financially. Have you ever tried living as a single person in a safe neighborhood in a military community? I haven't lived near family in years, so this constant running and chasing to serve in a leadership role, *looking* and at times *feeling* more like a client, wore me down. I was full of stress and worries that I never want to know again. Despite my struggle, I couldn't wallow in the blame game, and I decided to accept 100 percent responsibility for myself. This belief helped me to change my perception of approaching life and work.

I tried everything I knew to increase my finances because, as far as I could see, that was the root of my problem. I earned another degree and CEUs, stayed late, created more, and gave everything. I added more and more roles and hats because I was solely responsible for ensuring that I had a roof over my head. I remember a sorority sister telling me that I was a roadrunner, and another friend from college sharing that I "never" made time for them anymore. It was true, and it was also hurtful, but I was too busy trying to recover and survive that I missed missing them—until I looked up one day, and no one was around.

Who was I supposed to ask for help? What were my options? My relationships suffered, and I grew accustomed to handling everything alone.

I moved on to the next idea of how to adult, submitting over three hundred resumes in one year. I had an interview at a company I knew nothing about for a position I was nowhere near qualified for, but I went anyway. (I didn't get the job.) I changed industries once more, and I decided to start my first business. I promised myself I would never again do the kind of work that caused the burning anxiety in my chest because it was so powerfully soul-sucking. (I had literally traded my soul to survive. I don't recommend betraying yourself at all, obviously, but especially in that way.)

I needed something—but what? I had a financial problem, but I also needed to *shift my belief.* I needed to see myself differently. I needed to *close the gap* between who I was and who I believed myself to be. I couldn't show up for others if I wasn't able to show up for myself, so I had to remember who I was before busy and isolation became a way of life. I had to shift into a new version of myself, and in that new version, I had to *reclaim my identity*—one that did not include a title or a role.

I know it's a lot, but I'd be doing you a disservice if I skipped over the hard parts and the years of fumbling and stumbling I experienced. People often assumed I possessed some superpower that made me superhuman and unable to *feel*. Unless we were close friends, you would have never known I was suffering, because even in my worst moments, I still gave extraordinarily. I again felt obligated to finish, and to finish well. It was an effort to still "give it all you've got" in hopes of something being the one thing that would finally allow me to rest.

I almost drowned twice as a kid. The first time was at a park where I was way too excited to get in the water for the first time. Zeal is still sometimes a challenge for me, by the way. Still, the approach of jumping into the deep end of the water is how I felt about going into my career and entrepreneurship. I'd earned a few degrees, and I knew how to sharpen my technical skills. Still, I was too busy surviving and missed making fundamental changes within myself.

So, while I wasn't drowning in the literal sense, I was figuratively during those times in my life. There are extensive periods, particularly in my twenties, that I have no memory of whatsoever—they're simply a blur. I was treading water in theory, doing the doggy paddle for years before I learned the butterfly stroke. In real life, in my fundamental shift, I perfected my swim stroke, and I also decided to *step out of the water*.

I don't wear tenacity as a badge of honor; it is merely a part of my experience. When I could finally slow down and embrace peace, I gained clarity on my values, motivation, and unhealthy perspective on self-reliance. I identified my weaknesses. But I was determined to scale this mountain, so I went through an immersive experience of forgiveness and release. I surrendered to God's will in a way where I was no longer self-reliant and a protector of self. I remembered who I was and what I overcame. I remembered *why*. It wasn't a question of "What can I do?" but rather "*Why* do you do what you do?"

If you, too, find yourself seeking and blundering at the base of a mountain, you may want to ask yourself the same question. My story highlights a few work experiences that forcefully propelled me into being a solo entrepreneur. I noticed a theme in work environments, but I also had great experiences and met amazing people along my journey. During those times, I waited for permission from someone when I truly needed permission from myself *to myself*. I encourage you to consider that, too—*are you waiting for approval?*

I faced my fears more than once. In permitting myself to slow down and be still, I was completely isolated; no more busy, no more distractions, no more assignments. Faced with time and memories, I was able to explore parts of myself I'd previously pushed away, like my fear of abandonment and rejection. I'd experienced those things outside of myself, resulting in disappointment and severe loss. But I encountered those things within myself, too. I also uncovered a fear of failure.

In my pursuit of "Why?" I traded abandoning and rejecting myself for self-compassion, self-love, and self-acceptance. And once I fully understood my identity, I was able to reclaim my power. I shifted my money story. I defined success for myself, and I evaluated my "sunk costs." It was a pivotal moment of self-awareness, and I encourage you to spend time in your journal to assess your own.

In my work, I learned to operate in excellence and be present right now. I also learned that some criticism is subjective, and as long as you have done your best, it's okay to not always align with others on a decision. So, I encourage you to stick with what brings you joy unless it doesn't make fiscal sense—and even then, you may find that it eventually does. I highly recommend operating in your area of genius, outsourcing, and hiring early. You want to keep a good group of people surrounding you.

I quietly experienced extreme misfortune in unbelievable circumstances. I have survived things that should have killed me or at least broken me. I have been quite bruised, but never broken. When I decided to move from ocean depths to mountain peaks, I understood I could repeatedly scale a mountain. (I have experience running up hills with medicine bags. I do not, however, have expertise in climbing an actual mountain.) I do not know what it feels like to give up, but I know misplaced tenacity feels like depression. It is new to me to be vulnerable, welcome support, ask for help, and allow clearance. Still, I imagine that vulnerability has a place in embracing being tenacious.

One of my favorite scriptures is Romans 12:2: "Do not conform to the pattern of this world but be transformed by the renewing of your mind." You may ask me why this quote wasn't at the beginning of my story. The answer is that life happens, and it's easy in hindsight to simplify "becoming." But until you walk a difficult road or face deep pain, it can be challenging to resonate with simplicity.

Renewing my mind triggered the shift in my vision. When I didn't believe for myself or in myself, I leaned on my mother's belief. You need an overcomer mindset to go from base camp to the peak, from valley experiences to mountaintops. And as weak as you may feel when climbing in the thick of winter, you need the power to climb. Work your belief muscles, your creativity muscles, and your tenacious muscles. Then, to climb your mountain, follow the guideposts, and as you move along, create flow.

What happens the closer you get to a mountain peak? There is a natural tendency to lose momentum on the way up. If you are tired, worn, or weary, and you know you need to finish, know that I hear you. I urge you to consider your "why." Your "why" is your reason and is unrelated to monetary gain or any outside forces. If you are extrinsically motivated, you may be motivated by money, titles, others' attention, or anything other than doing the work. But suppose you are like me, and intrinsically motivated. In that case, you reap satisfaction from knowing you completed the job and gave your best effort.

If you want to cultivate tenacity, ask yourself how you define and measure your self-worth, self-value, and self-efficacy. You also want to clarify "why." When I first operated as a business owner, I quickly learned that money wasn't enough for me—your "why" determines if you finish and how you finish.

The world needs your influence, and there is someone out there who needs your story and your experience. They need you to permit yourself to show up. After I redefined success for myself—navigated through fears, failure, and loss—I gained the greatest gift of a renewed perspective. I now operate from a place of heart-centered work, which means that I am clear on my purpose and its value in the world. I changed my environment, reestablished boundaries and expectations, got clear on my "why," and laser-focused on my personal growth. I did the work, sorting out unaddressed grief. I developed non-negotiables in my morning routine and set boundaries around my time. And before I contributed to the growth and launch of anyone else, I focused on myself. I now live a self-care lifestyle and rest, and I routinely unplug from the demands of work and business to simply enjoy life. I am a change agent who loves helping busy creatives, leaders, and change-makers excel in life and work.

You can do the impossible when you commit to yourself. The time will pass by anyway—what will you do with it?

About the author: Felicia Ford is a growth strategist, catalyst, philanthropist, and advocate. She cultivates a multi-platform experience for busy creatives, leaders, and change-makers to excel in life and business, rooted in positive psychology and habit.

Felicia believes that the intersection of life and work or work and life should exist as an experience where we find joy in the creation and the delivery. Her purpose is to help others create experiences, so they can fully show up in all of their glory…and make others FEEL it.

She is also the executive director of a private philanthropic foundation and an agency fellow with the Center for Education Policy Research at Harvard University.

You can find her latest projects at www.feliciafordandco.com or on Instagram at @friendscallmefe.

Connection

by Kacie Steinmetz

When I was a teenager, I would often vacation with my mom and stepdad. On these trips, I'd go out on the beach by myself, weaving romantic fantasies of my future. I'd dream about meeting a man who would want to walk on the beach with me at night. He would brush the hair back from my face before gently taking me in his arms under the full moonlight.

Perhaps I read too many Danielle Steel romances back then—I certainly had high expectations! It's always a full moon, isn't it? And I've never met a man who values a gentle caress on the cheek as much as my girlfriends and I do! It's such a tender gesture!

I feel like I've spent a lifetime of not-so-amazing relationships searching for the one that would fit the way I'd imagined adult relationships should be. Our brains are hardwired to crave the bliss of first love, connecting to another human so deeply that we are driven by a powerful and addictive hormonal cocktail that actually changes our body's physiology. It helps us see past our partner's potential flaws or differences (read: incompatibilities) and see them in such a way that we are ensured to create a bond and make a commitment. This is part of the perfect human design to secure the survival of our species.

But I was addicted to the cocktail and painfully unaware that romantic love always fades and hormones level off. Couples are confronted with difficult situations (remember those overlooked incompatibilities) that require the same level of commitment *without* the romance-induced gaga goggles. I had no idea as a young woman that this was a "fact of life," and that the cocktail buzz was always going to wear off!

I got married at the ripe old age of twenty-six. The cocktail buzz really wasn't ever that intense for me, but I felt like I was making a safe choice. Being the younger child of divorced parents, the safe choice seemed like the smart choice. I wasn't particularly challenged to do better or be better; I could coast and still be taken care of by someone who seemed to be grateful to be with me. But based on my teenage fantasy, it would have seemed unlikely that I would have chosen to marry a man simply because he made me feel secure. Those fairy tale expectations were high! He was nothing like the hopeless romantic I'd always dreamed about!

But is it really a mystery why we do anything at twenty-six? My body clock was ticking, I'd been in more failed relationships than Liz Taylor, and I was scared of being alone forever. My older brother wasn't married, either, and my mom desperately wanted grandchildren someday. (Maybe that was *her* clock I heard ticking.) I jumped into something I was less than sure of at the time, but I really wanted to feel like I was someone else's number one. And before the wedding, I would have said he wasn't perfect, but he was perfect for me, and I just knew he could make me happy.

At first glance, that might not seem like a high expectation. But we are never really anyone else's number one, and that is as it should be. It was never his job to make me happy; that was—and is—my job exclusively. Someone else's happiness is too much responsibility for anyone. (Hint: Because it's a long-term impossibility.)

Psychologist and award-winning author and speaker Dr. John Gottman states that, "Couples spend year after year trying to change each other's minds—but it can't be done. This is because most of their disagreements are rooted in fundamental differences of lifestyle, personality, or values, which often go ignored during that 'puppy love' stage." It's like an evil joke nature plays on humans, but once those hormonal cocktails wear off, and the sobering reality of day-to-day habits and decisions takes over, the strength of our human relationships remains monumentally important—not just to living a "happy life," but to living a healthy and thriving one!

I genuinely believed I wasn't trying to change his mind, but our marriage certainly began to wear down after the births of our two children. Once the pleasantries faded and we were both using the bathroom with the door open, there still should have been that spark of simply enjoying each other's company and sharing hard emotions and decisions. We had a terrible disconnect that way. We were tag-teaming the kids and household duties and never meeting on a level deeper than a quickie before I fell into an exhausted sleep and he got up to watch TV or play around on his computer—or maybe work, I never really knew.

I wanted someone in the bed next to me. I needed someone emotionally present enough to validate my feelings. I wanted an equal partnership, and not just hearing what he thought I wanted to hear, then doing what he wanted. As a high extrovert, I would desperately want to feed off his energy, but he was never particularly vulnerable or tender with me. Though I've never actually considered this until now, I believe that was a huge part of the death of our relationship.

It was ten years before I gave up, because I didn't know what my other options were. I'd been to counseling. *We'd* been to counseling. I'd read books (or started books) on how to be a better wife, how to better respect my husband.

The disconnect remained. It was a gap so big that seemingly neither of us could jump across it.

It is in our best interest, both as individuals and for the greater good of our communities and our world at large, to nurture deep and meaningful relationships, far beyond the euphoria of romance and lust. It is in the space of community, within our immediate families and beyond, that we learn about ourselves and where we fit, identify our purpose, and subsequently develop our best selves. From there, we should all strive to bring our best selves to our most valued and important relationships—but at this point in my life, I also recognize that we are built up not just by the strength of our most important relationships, but also the lack thereof.

I agree with Dr. Henry Cloud, who states in his book, *The Power of the Other*, that *meaningful* relationships "sustain the physical connections hardwired in the brain…it is in relationships that our minds are actually built." I knew in my heart that my marriage could not have been defined as a meaningful relationship. It was an important one, of course, as it played a huge role in my everyday life, but there was something missing that was so monumental, it had become a detriment to both of us. I didn't want to be married to a roommate, and I didn't actually want to feel safe. I wanted *connection*.

Somehow we missed the lesson about how to connect and communicate when life got hard. And at twenty-six, I wasn't authentic with myself and didn't really know what I wanted. It was hard to define what connection meant to me at the time. I knew I wanted someone who knew how to touch me—holding my hand in public, sensing when I was tense and rubbing my shoulders, a kiss in the morning, a kiss goodnight, a kiss when greeting or before separating from each other. (I do love kissing!) I knew that physical touch wasn't his love language, but I assumed that because he was a man, he would love to touch me and be near my body. This was a huge deficit, and I didn't know how to communicate the importance of it.

I also didn't know that I wanted him to argue with me and fight fair, not stoop to name-calling or shaming or gaslighting when I had actual emotions that weren't pretty. I didn't know that I desperately wanted him to acknowledge the things that were important to me and be willing to explore them with me, like attending church, being on a lifelong self-awareness journey, and exploring all kinds of personal development. I had no idea that these types of connection were even missing, so I didn't know how to fix them. How do you bridge a gap you can't see?

The answer is, you don't—you just walk into it a hundred times a day and wonder how you keep falling flat on your face every time.

Dr. Cloud also stated that "the invisible attributes of relationship, the *connections* between people, have real, tangible, and measurable power...they have stronger immune systems, tend to get sick less frequently, and recover faster." They also live longer and succeed with their goals at a greater rate.

I was trying to work toward whatever goals I had set for myself, but I was struggling. I was low energy and high stress, and I felt angry all the time. We had no common goals—I'd given up on that. I had, in fact, given up on working things out at all, because it just took too much energy. I danced around issues to avoid conflict, because the surrender was deadly.

I will never forget the day I fell to my knees behind my bed, knowing that if I wanted to become the person I knew I was, I had to be free of this relationship that I felt held me back. It was within a couple of days that I penned the letter saying I wanted something more than we had, though I didn't specifically ask for a divorce.

He packed up his things and left. As if he'd been expecting it.

Unfortunately, I didn't realize any of my truths until after we divorced.

The idea that meaningful relationships contribute to the health of the brain and the body was compelling enough to encourage extra effort in my pursuit of a meaningful relationship. I wanted someone to work toward positive encounters when things got tough, not turn on me in anger with unsupported accusations about how I ruined every good thing with a bad mood. And though it's perfectly natural to want to give up in the midst of a heated conflict, it isn't a choice to be taken lightly in the long term. What "giving up" actually means has to be examined individually, because often the damage control that potentially follows isn't worth letting the conflict get the best of the relationship.

Surrendering to conflict in a way that is decidedly defeated is similar to giving up on the relationship itself; it's important to make conscious choices about what specifically is being surrendered. I am most assuredly not referring to relationships that are grossly out of balance with regard to respect and basic courtesies, or that are consistently or frequently in unhealthy conflict, which of course includes verbal, emotional, and physical abuse. Though I personally couldn't identify these traumatic conditions in my own marriage, it was most definitely out of balance. However, it *is* important for healthy, happy couples to recognize that conflict is an integral part of growth in a relationship. This is the type of conflict to which I am referring—this is what makes relationships stronger.

There are some basic, foundational elements that help determine whether two people are basically compatible. By compatible, I mean two people who can live in the same house (or even in the same "world," for couples who are separated by distance), who work toward similar and/or completely unrelated goals, and who still show affection, admiration, appreciation, or respect (or any combination therein) toward each other for an extended length of time and on a consistent basis. I don't believe soulmates exist as defined by *one* person for every person; it's the couples who *want* their relationship to thrive and who commit to doing whatever it takes who are soulmates. The ones who *make* it happen. I believe *that* is compatibility, but ultimately, relationships are multifaceted and utterly complicated. If two people are willing to put in the effort and want similar things in life, there's an excellent chance for ongoing intimate and genuine connection. Even if only one person wants a shift in the relationship, then change and growth is still possible, though it may be a slower, more difficult process.

I still believe in the power of being invested in the most important relationships in my life and holding strong to the hope of growing and enriching my understanding of how to communicate and love authentically. As a coach, I believe it can be a reality for everyone, which might sound like I'm talking from both sides of my mouth. Clearly I didn't hold strong; I didn't know how to love more authentically. And after a lot of self-study, a couple bad decisions, and a whole lot of trying to connect, I chose disconnection. I weighed my options and felt that it was the right thing for me and my family—not an easy choice or a desired choice, but it *was* the next step of a really hard leg of our journey.

Within a year after our separation, I met the man who would become my second husband. We took things slow and recognized that having failed marriages behind us could work against us in many ways, but the level of awareness was so much higher that we were able to relate to one another on a whole different level.

In his book, *Getting the Love You Want: A Guide for Couples*, Dr. Harville Hendrix breaks down the characteristics of a conscious partnership. Some of the attributes are being honest about your strengths and abilities, as well as the ones you lack; learning how to get your own needs met and valuing their needs almost as much as you do your own; and seeing and accepting your partner for who they are and how they may not always be able to help you meet your needs.

I found myself in a tailspin during and after a visit to a local theme park that we took with our combined four children. Very close in age, but very different in personalities, we found ourselves going in different directions with different children. When my expectation for where we should be meeting at whichever appointed time conflicted with his, I became very anxious—paralyzed, even. I was most likely with the youngest of the four—my biological daughter—and I can only remember with regret how I must have checked out on her, because I was so worried about when we were going to meet up again. It more than likely put a huge damper on everyone's enjoyment of the park and of the day.

It wasn't until much later that night that I realized my paralysis was something that had originated years earlier from circumstances in my first marriage—which I can now acknowledge may have actually started with the departure of my own dad when I was three.

It's vital to be intentional and thoughtful about how you communicate what you need and take ownership of your role in the success of the relationship. We are so much better in relationships when we know ourselves first—recognizing our triggers, our strengths and abilities, our needs, our fears, and our limitations. How did it take me so long to admit that something that happened thirty-five years prior was still affecting my relationships today? It was a huge moment. This man who was my new boyfriend at the time had never hurt me, never abandoned me, and yet he was being punished over events of my life that had nothing to do with him!

Dr. Hendrix also noted, "In a conscious partnership you realize you have to *be* the right partner… A good relationship requires commitment, discipline, and the courage to grow and change; creating a fulfilling love relationship is hard work." It's important, he notes, to "see your partner not as your savior, but as another wounded human being, struggling to be healed."

Compatibility isn't doing *what* the other person wants; it's about being someone *you want to be* with someone who *wants you to be that person, too*!

I was ready to be the person I wanted to be, and I could tell that he could see the qualities in me that I had *hoped* to reflect. And it isn't that he helped make me who I am—it's that he supported who he knew I had the potential to be, and as a result, I've been able to flourish, feeling safe and valued in a relationship with another healthy human being! Since meeting Matt, current husband extraordinaire, I've completed my yoga teacher training program, a life coaching certification program, and purchased a yoga studio! I always knew I wanted to help people, but I never knew how I was supposed to do that. The challenges and disconnection that I faced in my first marriage led me, eventually, into the clearest vision of who I was at the deepest level of me.

It all sounds very romantic, but the reality is that relationships are hard! Families are hard, life is hard, and we are no exception. We argued over the silliest thing just last night, but we've both gotten so much better about letting go of judgment about who's "right" and who's "wrong," and taking some ownership in any conflict or uncomfortable situation. It has made a world of difference! I'm still learning how to let go of assumptions about someone else's intentions, and when I ask questions, I try to allow myself to be led by curiosity instead of the crazy stories I tell myself. (This is a huge step in relating to people outside my marriage as well!) If we can be curious about our own triggers and responses as well as our partner's, it can help in finding compassion during a time of high emotion and disagreement.

Curiosity and compassion for yourself *and* your partner-in-conflict is an excellent way to diffuse a high-tension situation.

We are all energetic beings, and our energy is felt by others, whether we or they realize it! When we choose our attitude from a place of affection or respect or just plain curiosity, it shifts the perspective and releases *our* attachment to any expectations or possible disappointments. Once we do that, we've made space for others to join us in a more positive place—a more authentically connected place.

No matter the mate you choose for yourself, it's important to be your own number one—knowing who you are at your core, knowing your own triggers, knowing the way you communicate and understand expressions of affection. No one can make you happy if *you* don't know how. People in authentic relationships are willing to work *on and for* themselves, as well as working with (but not *on*—see the difference?) their spouses. If you don't know who you are and what you want, how can you know if another person aligns with that?

We all have that inner knowing that tells us when we're giving too much value to something (or someone) that doesn't deserve it. If you're wasting energy engaging in unhealthy or pointless conflict, or lingering in a relationship that doesn't feel authentic and healthy, don't ignore your instincts. It's important to give weight to that inner knowing, before *or* after you're established in a relationship. It's okay to be nervous about committing to a new love or be angry at your partner over a disagreement; not every day is a fairy tale or a picnic when you share your whole life with another person. It's natural to take that seriously and have some nervous excitement or passionate emotion. It is not, however, natural to feel undervalued or minimized. If you are not the best version of yourself with the person to whom you're committed, then there should be a question mark around the issue which makes you feel inadequate. But keep in mind that the question mark may be yours, and not your partner's. It's important to accept that genuine connection and lasting love relationships take work, but they should not be consistently painful or out of balance.

I *love* love, just the same now as I did when I was a teenager. I'm a hopeless romantic, and even though things didn't work out for me the first time around, I have finally found a man who will take me out on the beach at night and hold my hand in the moonlight. (He's still not a cheek caresser, but that's worth overlooking with this one.) Part of the deal—which was not included in the fantasy—is the fact that we take the kids, too, so they can chase sand crabs. But if the moon is out and my guy is there, then that's surely where I want to be! I've come to embrace that nothing is ever perfect, including us, and we certainly miss the mark as often as we hit it when it comes to settling conflict. But we've both committed to doing the work and honoring each other's vulnerabilities. We don't use the intimate things we know about each other as weapons, and we're learning how to back off and regroup when the tension is high and the crocodile brain has taken over. Most importantly—the real game-changer—we took time to know ourselves and to genuinely know each other first, and the level of connection is unbreakable. When two partners are both "all in," it's a force that's unstoppable.

That is my hope for you—that you can find connection and be "all in" with someone who matches your level of passion and commitment to the union. That you have found or will find someone with whom you can be authentic, aligned, and fully invested. Take the time to know yourself and define what brings you joy, and what your aspirations are for life and relationships. And as crazy as this life is, at the fast pace we travel, I hope you find the opportunity to be present and joyful with your loved ones in spite of chaos or conflict. May God bless you and your relationships!

About the author: Kacie Steinmetz is a relationship coach and owner of Shine Yoga in Virginia Beach, Virginia. She received a yoga teacher certification in 2005 and a life coaching certification from Coach Training Alliance in 2013. One of her core beliefs is that feeling well in body and confident in spirit leads to more genuine connection, respectful communication, and joy in relationships. She helps people who are in complicated or difficult relationships—personal and professional—learn to communicate authentically and purposefully.

She is also a Richway Amethyst BioMat and BioAcoustic Mat distributor and reiki practitioner. Aside from raising teenagers, small business ownership has been her greatest learning curve and most joyous endeavor!

When Kacie isn't blessed with an abundance of activity with her husband and four children, she enjoys music performance, reading, and traveling.

You can find her latest projects at www.kaciesteinmetz.com and www.shineyogavabeach.com.

Reinvention

by Erin Klein

It was a hot day in June as I sat inside fantasizing about lying by a pool with a cold drink. That was quite possibly my favorite pastime. I could sit in the sun for hours as long as I had a pool to cool off in and an empowering book that would help me with achieving my goals.

My daydream was interrupted by my phone ringing. I rushed to answer it, as I was so excited for a conversation with another adult. It was my mentor, and this usually meant that I was about to be super empowered, inspired, and ready to take on the world.

This time was different. Instead of getting off the phone and feeling that surge of invincibility, I felt left out, alone, and falling behind.

See, I had recently given birth to a seven-pound, eight-ounce bundle of joy—Connor. While this was a wonderful and thrilling occasion, the aftermath left me confused and questioning who I was and what my purpose on this earth was. I listened as my friend gave me the good news about his recent deals, his new ideas that were being brought to fruition, and how he was taking the world by storm. He was succeeding at a high level, and while I was happy for him, I was quietly questioning my own worth, ability, and skills. It wasn't necessarily the competition, but seeing my business remain stagnant that was a shot to my identity and my whole being. I was watching others flourish from the sidelines, while I was up all night and trying to keep up with the bare necessities of life—forget growing and thriving.

I got off the phone and stared outside. My thoughts were soon overtaken by the cries of a six-week-old baby who needed his mom. It instantly brought tears to my eyes.

I went through a whirlwind of emotions during those fifteen seconds. I felt guilty that I wasn't practicing gratitude for success in my businesses. I felt angry that I was stuck inside on a beautiful day. I felt frustrated that my baby was crying and I didn't know why. I felt insignificant to the outside world. I felt overwhelmed by all of these thoughts, and I felt like the worst mother in the entire world.

I spent the rest of the day taking care of my son and trying to find the words to articulate to my husband how I was feeling. I wasn't usually the best at that. I would get worked up and start yelling and slamming doors. Those events were typically followed by feelings of remorse and confusion. I didn't understand what was happening to me and why I seemed to be losing my mind. I had heard people talk about postpartum depression, but I would immediately rule that out when it came to myself. There was no way that someone like me, who had spent fourteen years on personal growth and development, could fall into something like that! Impossible, right?

Before I went to bed that night, I wrote down an idea. It might be the entrepreneurial part of my brain that gives me the need to find solutions to problems, but I knew there was no way I was alone in my feelings about motherhood. This idea would soon become the catalyst for getting myself out of this funk and igniting a new fire within me. I knew there had to be other women who felt confused about their identities and roles in life after having a baby. I couldn't be the only one who was battling these thoughts and trying to rediscover my purpose. Surely other moms also felt guilty about their desires to create and to thrive in life outside of the home.

I decided that I needed to be around other moms. I needed to get out of the house more and interact with people who were in similar situations. And each time I heard another mom tell a story or talk about an issue they were dealing with, I felt encouraged. I was right—I wasn't alone. I started realizing that the feelings I had were *valid*. I wasn't losing my mind, and if other women could thrive in businesses and other areas in life with kids, then there was absolutely no reason why I couldn't as well.

This wasn't an instant turnaround. I struggled at times, and to be completely honest, I still have moments of struggle. I'm sure I'm not alone in the fact that I can take a molehill and turn it into a mountain in my head at lightning speed. I used to be able to just hop in my car and go for a drive or go shopping when I felt overwhelmed, but that's not so easy to do with a baby at home. I would often feel stuck—as if no matter what was happening, I was powerless to change anything because I was chained to this tiny person all the time.

The only thing I knew for certain was that I was in control of how I reacted in these scenarios. Instead of beating my head against a wall and feeling hopeless, I took a moment to breathe and put things into perspective. I took the time to realize that in the overall grand scheme of life, my baby whining and wanting to be picked up wasn't really that terrible. I reminded myself that he wasn't always going to want his mommy to sit on the floor and play with him, and I owed it to both of us to be there in the moment. Then I thought about how many moms would love to be able to be home with their babies more, and that I was fortunate to have that chance.

Gratitude has played a big role in embracing this new life and the new identity that I'm creating.

As for my businesses, I made some tweaks and found ways to still feel fulfilled in doing the things I loved. I knew if I wanted to be a good mom and a successful businesswoman, I needed to prioritize my values. I needed to understand my triggers so that I could come up with a plan to handle the inevitable meltdowns. I knew that I began to feel stressed when I had ideas or tasks to complete, but was unable to focus because of my little one. To counter that, I keep post-its everywhere. I write everything down, so I don't forget—and when it's my son's naptime, I attack those notes.

I have had to up my level of communication with my husband. My first mistake was thinking he was a mind-reader, but he most definitely is not. I had to speak up and be clear about how I was feeling and what I needed. We both keep busy with business, church, and coaching sports, so we sat down and developed a schedule that allowed us to still do things that kept us happy and gave us time away from home.

The biggest lesson I have learned on this journey of creating a harmonious new identity as a mom and businesswoman (among the many other hats that moms can wear) is self-love and grace. I have had to look myself in the mirror and tell myself the following: *You* are important. *You* still matter. *You* need to make sure you do things that still make you feel happy, fulfilled, and good about yourself.

These days, I am not moving nearly as fast as I would like to, and I'm learning that it's okay. I feel like I am on this path and have a desire to help other moms who have this feeling. If something is heavy on my heart, I act on it. I make sure it aligns with who I am as a person. Because when we are living in our truths, it makes life a whole lot more enjoyable. And my truth is that sometimes life gets messy, but it's always manageable.

This isn't the death of an old, powerful me, but rather the birth of a new woman who is growing every day. A woman I get to reinvent and redefine. It's a new journey of discovery with a little sidekick. I am a work-in-progress and a masterpiece, all at the same time! So, I have decided to embrace this new life as a chance to inspire other moms and let them know they're not alone, and that they don't have to give up on who they are in order to fit the mold of a "good mom."

Never let titles or changes take you off the course of who you are and what you're meant to do. You are powerful and can take charge of your life in any way that you like. Challenges help us grow and give us the opportunity to reinvent ourselves!

About the author: Erin is an entrepreneur, coach, and speaker. She is the founder of Moms Just Wanna Have Sun and host of *The Confident Woman* podcast.

She started down her entrepreneurial path in 2006 after changing majors every semester in college. She ended up finding her stride and happiness in the travel space because of her desire to see the world.

Her mission is to help moms maintain their badass, goal-crushing selves as they take on motherhood. Erin loves sports, and so in addition to her businesses, she is a girls' basketball coach. She uses her time to give back and find ways to empower others to start living in their passion and get out of their own way.

You can find her latest projects at www.momsjustwannahavesun.com or on Instagram at @erin_travelsforlife.

Now, write your story...

Use this page to write your story. Your message and your story deserve to be told. And we hope you choose The Rising Sisterhood as your beacon.

If you are ready, we would love to have you as part of our Rising Sisterhood movement. Go here for more information: therisingsisterhoodbook.com/coauthor

A Special Thanks to Our Contributors

First and foremost, I want to recognize and thank the contributors to this book, *The Rising Sisterhood*. Nothing is more powerful than a badass woman who courageously believes in herself and her ability to fiercely impact the world—except for a whole tribe of sisters.

We are truly a sisterhood.

These ladies dove into the deep end with me, and I am truly grateful to lock arms with them in this powerful movement.

I encourage you to surround yourself with women who support, empower, encourage, and celebrate each other. Be among women who are dedicated to learning, growing, embracing, and owning their authentic selves.

Never underestimate the powerful shift that occurs when you align with beautiful, ambitious souls who are running alongside you on the journey of creating and living your best lives.

Cassie Kitzmiller	Charmaine Johnson-Fuller
Christine Lu Singh	Erin Klein
Felicia Ford	Giselle Grant
Hannah Hassler	Jillian Bright
Kacie Steinmetz	Kayleigh Hanlin
Lucy Liu	Michele Duhigg
Rachel Smets	Sharon White
Tonia Rolle Jones	

Acknowledgments

To my husband, David—without your gentle "push," I'm not sure I would have felt so safe in sharing my story. You are my rock, my biggest cheerleader, and my favorite partner-in-crime.

To my family, for allowing me time to write—and also for your patience, while I listened to the *Hamilton* soundtrack on repeat to let my creative juices flow.

To my team, who encourages, empowers, and supports me in creating a business that is built upon crafting systems for other impact-driven entrepreneurs.

I'd also like to say a special thank you to Stephenie Surber, my project coordinator, who helped to craft this vision and was there as a sounding board throughout this project.

To the entire book team, thank you for lending your genius and expertise to the cover, the layout, and the edits. Your support and guidance has truly shaped this book.

To the women in my community, thank you for your tough love and creativity during this process. You were a driving force on the days when imposter syndrome tried to creep in.

Join the Sisterhood Collective

The Rising Sisterhood is so much more than a book. It's a community. A mission. A movement. It's the Rising Sisterhood Collective, a membership site for women dedicated to rise and support each other.

The membership includes amazing features like:
- monthly journal prompts
- monthly affirmations
- monthly workshop with guest speakers
- new resources delivered each month
- exclusive sisterhood community
- monthly collaboration opportunities
- 15% discount on co-authoring opportunities

Imagine feeling guided and supported when you're struggling or feeling alone or overwhelmed.

Imagine being able to reach out to other womxn who have faced similar challenges and risen above them with grace and grit.

PLUS each of the authors is sharing an incredible gift for members inside the Collective!

Ready to join the Collective?
Head here > therisingsisterhoodbook.com/collective

Don't Forget to Leave a Review!

Every review matters, and it matters a *lot*!
Head over to Amazon or wherever you purchased this book to leave a review,
then tag us at @therisingsisterhoodbook.

Why leave a review?

Aside from showing Amazon's algorithm that we are indeed a legit book, you let other potential readers know if this book is worth it for them. If you found inspiration, joy, wisdom, motivation, encouragement, community, or hope from any of our stories, please consider taking a few minutes to let other potential readers know your thoughts and feelings about *The Rising Sisterhood*.

The Rising Sisterhood thanks you endlessly.

Made in the USA
Monee, IL
11 March 2021